becoming me

CHOOSING TO BE YOU

EMILY B. CUMMINS

Published by BecomingMe.TV, LLC

Paperback ISBN 979-8-9852742-0-2
Hardback ISBN 979-8-9852742-1-9
eBook ISBN 979-8-9852742-2-6

Italics in Scripture quotations reflect the author's added emphasis.

Cover and interior design by Amanda Wolfe, Growco Lab
Edited by Emily Sison, Allie Reefer, Marisa Angelino, Caitlyn Pace, Michael Allen
First Edition May 2022

www.becomingme.tv

For Team Cummins—thank you for always challenging & encouraging me to become who God made me to be.

For you, warrior friend—this book is a reflection of my becoming journey, and my prayer is that it becomes a source of encouragement on your becoming journey, too. I'm cheering you on big time as you're becoming who God made you to be!

table of contents.

forward. 9

introduction. 11

love yourself. 15

at the well. 17

confession:
sometimes i struggle with discouragement. 23

lessons learned from kidney stones. 27

hope and healing in addiction. 35

what do you need to leave behind? 39

why i didn't think i was beautiful, until i did. 43

the day God hugged me in the starbucks
drive-through line. 47

the real story behind galentine's day. 51

6:00 a.m. friends. 55

becoming katie. 59

warrior steps. 63

choose to be her. 65

who do you want to be? 67

look what you made me do. 73

what's your why? 83

female. 87

table of contents.

expecting Jesus to show up. 91

experience is what you make it. 95

making lemonade. 99

becoming allie. 103

warrior steps. 107

warrior. 109

now i'm a warrior. 111

lacing up your warrior boots in peace. 115

rocky road ice cream is a lot like life. 125

becoming's a marathon, not a sprint. 127

moving forward after a break-up. 131

what happens when we allow the evil
in the world to become the evil in us? 137

when it feels like you're the only single person
in the world. 141

dear future husband. 145

fighting to become you. 147

becoming amanda. 153

warrior steps. 157

fail + fly. 159

more being, less doing. 161

table of contents.

the car jam session that checked my heart. 165

dear me: lessons learned. 169

when you feel uninvited. 173

being authentic in a filter-covered world. 177

friends & frenemies. 181

5-4-3-2-1-GO. 189

lionhearted faith. 193

becoming ana. 197

warrior steps. 207

your story matters. 201

we all have a story. 203

sharing your story. 207

how to talk about the hard parts of your story. 211

hope in the midst of tragedy. 215

warrior cheerleader. 219

i am becoming! 225

becoming allison. 229

warrior steps. 231

acknowledgements. 233

about the author. 237

forward.

In every book or journal my warrior Daddy has ever given me, he has always written a note in the front cover challenging, encouraging, equipping and inspiring me to BE who God uniquely designed me to be. I've asked him to write a note here to you, warrior friend, inviting you to choose to be who God made you to be, too.

The struggle is real. The pressure is intense. The battle between living as a human *being* or human *doing* is insane and leaves most of us worn out, confused, frustrated, and angry.

Social media promotes, "look at all I do," while privately we wrestle with who we really are becoming... or more accurately stated... who we are not becoming.

The gap between what I do and who I want to become widens and we sink further into despair—the energy to bridge the gap day after day between our "public persona" and "private reality" deepens, causing us to either give up on becoming who God created us to be, or feeling doomed to continue on in a "fake it 'til you make it" world.

There's good news: Emily B. Cummins pulls back the facade of her own life to reveal her inner tyranny of doing and becoming. *Becoming Me* exposes the distance between believing God and trusting God cannot be bridged by doing more, rather in becoming who God created you to be.

More than a book, this is Emily's life. At times satisfying, filled with promise and hope, only to turn towards scary and deeply disappointing and depressing during other seasons. How would I know this? Well... I've known her since day one, she's my daughter, and I thank God every day for choosing me to be her earthly father. She's gifted, not as in a Pinterest perfect life, but in the struggle to persevere in "becoming" who God created her to be.

Becoming Me is a trustworthy companion in your journey of moving past the facade of "doing"... towards a better life of "becoming"!

You've dreamed of living in this space... so...

Let the struggle to become begin.

ENJOY! Cheering you on,

Mark D. Cummins
"daddy to Emily"

December 1, 2021
Ocala, FL

introduction.

"All I ever wanted to be is who I'm becoming."

- Anonymous

Suffocation felt imminent. My earliest memories are truly happy memories, however, they're also laced with a devious undercurrent that threatened to sabotage who I was.

The "p" word haunted my thoughts—chasing perfection in my little girl ballet routines, middle school swim team competitions, high school SAT scores, college acceptance letters, and the selection of a college major. I chased perfection like a drug, always falling a few marks short, never quite the flawless ballerina, all-star swimmer, or A+ student.

No one placed this pressure on me; my pain was completely self-inflicted. Looking back, I now understand how much of my DNA and personality naturally led me to the breaking point (I'm an Enneagram 1, INTJ, and Owl, for all of you personality test gurus). However, my early twenty-something self felt like her world was crashing around her because she simply couldn't execute it perfectly.

I grew up in the church, in fact, my Daddy has been a pastor my entire life. I knew who Jesus was and never questioned whether I believed in Him, but in all my tear-filled doing and failing, I realized I didn't really know Jesus. Beginning my own relationship with God as a middle schooler—not assuming I had a relationship with Him because of my parents—ignited a life-changing invitation into freedom.

I found myself halfway through college on my knees before Jesus, choosing to trust Him with my story and relinquishing the false sense of control I had struggled to grasp. It was here, in my brokenness, that He extended the invitation to become who He had made me to be all along. God never designed me to be perfect, but to be becoming... learning, growing, falling down and getting back up, changing, and trying new things.

A saying from Shauna Niequist solidified this invitation in my heart and mind:

> This season is about becoming [...] walk closely with people you love, and with people who believe God is good and life is a grand adventure. Don't get stuck in the past, and don't try to fast-forward yourself into a future you haven't yet earned. Give today all the love and intensity and courage you can, and keep traveling honestly along life's path.
> (Shauna Niequest, *Bittersweet*)

In an instant, my worldview changed. For the first time, I truly believed the pursuit of perfection was futile and embarking on the life-long journey of becoming me was the greatest adventure I could start. To mark my moment, I tattooed that little eight-letter word on my wrist, putting in front of my eyes every single day the reminder that I'll never be perfect, I am becoming.

Warrior friend, you are becoming, too. I don't know your story, but I know God designed you on purpose, with purpose... to be uniquely you. Since getting that "becoming" tattoo on my wrist in 2012, my life has never been the same. I've embraced this adventure with gumption and a whole lot of grace. I've failed and fallen (a lot!), and in the falling, I've discovered that success is found in getting back up.

This is my prayer for you over the course of these pages. I pray you discover and believe that you, too, are becoming who God made you to be, and if you don't have a personal relationship with Jesus, you can begin a relationship with Him right now... it's as simple as praying something like this: *God, thank You for sending Your Son, Jesus, to die for me, and thank You that three days later He overcame death! I believe in you and trust You. Thank you for making me new. In Your Name I pray, amen.*

If you just made the decision to begin a personal relationship with God, welcome to the family! This is the most important decision you will ever make! I would love to celebrate with you—please email me at emily@becomingme.tv. This relationship is the foundation for the becoming journey and the only way to begin.

This book is a battle cry because becoming isn't a journey for the faint of heart. It's messy. It's hard. Most days I don't feel like lacing up my warrior boots and taking the next step in front of me. I have my fair share of anxiety, panic attacks, depression, doubt, fatigue, and anger. But I've tipped into this story... and I never want to go back to the slavery of perfection again. I've tasted freedom and won't give it up. That's my hope for you, too.

Know you're not alone here. My story along with Becoming Stories of hundreds of others are woven throughout this book—in fact, you'll be meeting one of my warrior friends at the end of each section in this book. So, grab a cup of coffee, and let's embark on this journey together... *becoming me.*

Cheering you on big time as you're becoming who God made you to be, warrior friend!

love yourself.

To become who you were made to be, you must first love yourself.

at the well.

"Flourish in every season."

- Julie Mullins

Moving to Las Vegas seven months after college graduation was my journey to the well. I carried my water jar of expectations, hopes and dreams, naively declaring, "God, this is the story I want to write. Let's go!" By His grace, Sin City became the bedrock for my choosing to become who He had made me to be all along.

Growing up a pastor's daughter, I had a squeaky clean reputation. Honor roll, church activities, and competing on the high school swim team crowned my resume like gold stars. I checked all the boxes on "success," continuing to strive for achievement throughout my college career.

Walking across the graduation stage at the University of Florida in May 2013, officially becoming a Florida Gator, I felt I had deplaned in unknown territory. Until that point, the expectations for success had been outlined for me—now, success was up to me, and I wasn't sure where to go next.

Diploma in hand, sifting job offers from multiple organizations in cities across the state of Florida, I battled direction, not knowing who I was or who I wanted to be without the bowling alley bumper guardrails guiding me in the right direction.

When I received a job offer from a church in the shiny city of Las Vegas, I was drawn to the glitz and glam... to a city that burned bright and stood in feisty boldness. Contrasting my internal identity struggle, I saw an opportunity to plant myself in a city oozing confidence.

In our stories, we only ever have rearview perspective to better understand why we made certain decisions or pursued different chapters. Looking back at this particular decision, I now know my twenty-two year old self moved for all the wrong reasons. However, I also see and firmly believe God's hand was on my becoming story in the midst of my less-than-best motives. Twenty-two year old Emily didn't know who she was or who she wanted to be, and when something glamorous invited her to join a mega plot twist, she couldn't help but resist. It was here, alone in a big city, that God taught me how to love myself.

In John 4, the Samaritan woman walking to the well had her own expectations and dreams, too. Life hadn't unpacked how she'd hoped, and with a string of failed relationships sticking to her reputation like glue, she was left alone.

I picture her walking in the heat of mid-day, sweat trickling down her arms as she lugged her water jar. Approaching the well, seeing a strange man, I sense her hesitancy and then boldness to move ahead and draw water, checking the box on her daily routine.

For this woman, it was here, in the desert, that God met her where she was—battling identity crisis, isolation, and the shame of her yesterdays. As Jesus invited her into conversation, He invited her to have an internal experience. He wasn't interested in satisfying her temporary need for water; He was ready to transform her from the inside-out. To receive this eternal water, she just needed to accept it.

The first two months after moving were the hardest. I was adjusting to everything being brand new—new community, new friends, new job, new house, new, new, new. And, within weeks,

I entered a dating relationship. Never having had a "boyfriend" before, when the first guy came knocking on my door, I didn't ask a lot of questions, but rather, dove in with both feet. Deep down, I knew nothing about dating this guy was right for me... the timing, who he was, and who I was becoming with him.

In the few weeks we dated, I focused on his potential rather than the actual truths of God. I clung to my water jar, falsely believing that if my relational need was satisfied, I would be satisfied. I would finally know who I was. But it was in having that temporary need met that I felt more lost than ever before. I isolated myself from my tribe and my community, I stopped writing, and I felt trapped inside the body of a person I didn't recognize.

If I was a fly on the wall in the Samaritan woman's story, I believe she would have felt somewhat similar. Trying desperately to satisfy needs externally, all the while draining herself of the light within. And in her encounter with Jesus, He took one look at her water jar—the hopes and expectations she desperately clung to—and said it would never satisfy her.

I was in a daze for weeks, unsure of what to do. Clinging to the relationship I had finally started, while knowing I needed to set down my water jar and embrace what God had for me.

In a breakthrough moment, I remember pulling into my workplace and parking my car. I was on the phone with my Daddy and decided today was the day... I was going to break-up with my water jar. After work, we met up at a local Starbucks, and in two minutes, I set my water jar down and waved goodbye to the very thing I hadn't been willing to trust God with in my story.

Driving away that night, I felt the fog literally lift. The next morning brought a fresh energy and passion I hadn't felt in weeks. I experienced God in a fresh way. I wrote. I cried. I thanked God for loving me enough to challenge me to set down the thing I thought would satisfy me, but never would.

This is what I love the most about my God. He writes the best stories. When God directed my steps in setting down my hopes, dreams, and expectations, He invited me into a journey I never thought I needed.

The following 22 months I spent living in Vegas after my water jar break up, I discovered what it meant to love myself. Growing up in church and having a personal relationship with Jesus for years, I had what I thought was respect for myself. I mean, I liked myself. I didn't hate who I saw in the mirror. But it wasn't until I clung to what wasn't best for me and found how hard it was for me to give it up, that I realized I didn't really—and I mean, really, deep down—love myself.

My becoming chapters in Las Vegas, far from my family and hometown, were when I was finally forced to get to know Emily. I didn't know what I was capable of until I was alone, empty handed, ready to receive what God wanted to do in me. In my own desert, God invited me to the well. He revealed how I had moved to a city in search of identity in career and relationships, but that I didn't need to have those titles to be valued. I was worthy all along only because He calls me worthy.

Remember that rearview mirror? Looking back at my 2014 and 2015 chapters, I traveled 2,000 miles to discover who I was, to experience the vast grace and love of a mighty God, and that becoming who He made me to be begins with really loving myself—and that can only happen when I know Him personally.

Those two years were marked by countless moments alone with Jesus, getting to know Him and His Word, trying things and failing a lot, learning that adventures on my own aren't "less than", finding out I'm a whole lot stronger than I thought I was, defining my own non-negotiables in life, and discovering that success is rooted solely in becoming who God made me to be... not in anything I accomplish or don't accomplish in this life.

The Samaritan woman leaving the well that day left her encounter with Jesus loving herself for the first time too. Leaving her water jar behind, she ran, declaring what Jesus had done for her. She proclaimed with her life what God had done in her, and what

He could do in those around her as well.

We can't leave an encounter with Jesus unchanged. Experiencing God and truly loving who He made you to be radiates from everything you do, from the center of who you are. As Jesus worked in me, I couldn't help but share my internal change with those around me, inviting friends to coffee and encouraging them to become who He made them to be, writing on my blog, posting on social media, and inviting friends to share their own Becoming Stories online, too.

Las Vegas, I ran to you for all the wrong reasons, but what Jesus did in my becoming story inside your gates won't just stay in Vegas. That once lost girl now knows who she is and who she's becoming... and she really loves herself!

confession: sometimes i struggle with discouragement.

"She was unstoppable. Not because she didn't have failures or doubts, but because she continued on despite them."
- Anonymous

It was a regular Monday morning, but I couldn't shake the icy grip of agitation clinging to my shoulders like a too-tight sweater. My emotions felt itchy, tingling with unanswered questions, changing seasons, and the fear that I just wouldn't measure up. I honed in on the uncomfortability. I took my eyes off of truth. And I lost sight of who God made me to be.

Some days I struggle with discouragement. I focus on what I don't know, on my failures and doubts, and simultaneously push pause on becoming the woman God made me to be. I'm learning in these moments that where I choose to fix my gaze determines whether I'll stand back up and continue on the journey, or stay down, embracing the posture of a defeated warrior.

Frustrating, irritating, and just downright yucky days will

come. Oh, warrior friend, they'll come. Days where mess-ups are made, favorite dishes broken, sweaters snagged, tires flattened, relationships jumbled, tempers flared, dreams altered, and goals left unaccomplished. And it's *okay*. These days are a part of this beautiful thing we call life. We need to embrace how we feel, but then choose to worship Jesus despite our temporary feelings. We must choose to stand up, shift our attention, and focus our eyes on the One who is greater than our current emotions, posture, thoughts, attitude, and circumstances.

I appreciate the example modeled by David throughout the book of Psalms. While one chapter depicts unbearable sorrow and unending grief, mere verses later, we find David praising Jesus wholeheartedly. And you know what's really cool? When David chooses to move from despair to praise, nothing has necessarily changed in his story—he doesn't have new answers to his situation or a set of fresh circumstances. He simply embraces his human feelings and then chooses to trust God with his emotions.

> Why am I discouraged?
> Why is my heart so sad?
> I will put my hope in God!
> I will praise Him again—my Savior and my God!
> (Psalm 42:5, NLT)

Hannah's story in 1 Samuel also resonates deeply with my heart's cry to fight the tendrils of discouragement and despair that attempt to derange my attitude, my posture, and who I choose to be. In 1 Samuel 1, we meet Hannah "crushed in soul" and begging God to relieve her pain, to hear her cries, and notice the anguish she has been drowning in. Here's the game-changing moment—as Hannah wept and embraced her broken heart, she prayed, sharing her emotions with Jesus. Then, standing up, Hannah left, "her face radiant" (1 Samuel 1:18, MSG). Hannah didn't leave with new answers or a different set of circumstances. She left her pain and requests at the feet of Jesus and her time with Him transformed her. She left a different woman, a woman not broken by her circumstances; a woman made whole through her trust in her Savior.

I want to walk with that kind of faith. At the end of the road, I want to be known as a woman who simply knew how to trust Jesus. And I don't want to only trust Him with the big things like who I'll marry or what else my future may hold. I want to trust Him wholeheartedly with the little things as well—the things that I try to control—the bad-hair-day-moments, the I-woke-up-on-the-wrong-side-of-the-bed mornings, and the I-really-need-more-coffee kind of afternoons. When my skin is crawling with agitation at the normal rhythms of life, I want to embrace that I may be frustrated and discouraged, but I don't have to live there. I will not live defeated. I want to live unstoppable.

> She was unstoppable. Not because she didn't have failures or doubts, but because she continued on despite them.
> (Anonymous)

She continued on despite them.

Hannah did. David did. And I want my story to say "Emily did" as well.

Discouraging days will come. What we do with them is what matters. Recognize how you feel and then choose where you place your hope—where you put your trust. What we do next with discouraging emotions is what matters, what shapes us, what helps us grow, and what helps us become.

nothing in
my story
takes God
by surprise.

lessons learned from kidney stones.

"Perhaps the butterfly is proof that you can go through a great deal of darkness yet become something beautiful."

- Anonymous

Moving to a new place comes with a laundry list of new things: new vehicle registration, new doctors offices, new dentists, new friends, new favorite restaurants, new grocery stores, new gas stations, new everything. Shortly after to my move to Las Vegas, the time came to tackle the "find a doctor" item on my to do list. So I did my research, asked a few friends, and landed on my best option. I dialed the number, made an appointment, and put a nice big check mark next to that line item. Check. One more item off the list.

And then I got sick.

And not just sick, but down-for-the-count, can't-get-out-of-bed, losing-track-of-days kind of sick. By the time the day of my appointment rolled around, I couldn't have been happier to have tackled that to-do list item the week before. I walked into my new doctor's office, conquered paperwork, went through the initial examinations, and then waited for the doctor's diagnosis.

"I'd like to get some x-rays and blood work done to check this out a little further," came her steady reply. "I think you potentially passed a kidney stone and I want to see if you have any other stones. You can get the x-ray taken care of today, and tackle the blood work tomorrow."

X-rays. No problem. That's practically like taking a nap. But blood work? Yikes. That wasn't something I was prepared for. Let me explain why...

In 2009, I had orthognathic jaw surgery. In a memorable turn of events, the surgery didn't go quite as planned and post-operation, I ended up in the ER dehydrated with nurses attempting to get an IV in my system. They tried 16 times before having any success. Just about every vein in my body was jabbed and poked as I pleaded with my own skin to cooperate. The second to last attempt was on the veins in my neck. I vividly remember being positioned so that my body was upside-down, blood rushing to my head, with the nurse trying to secure an IV needle. I don't think I've ever screamed as much as I did in those few moments. At one point, I remember my Daddy, staring straight into my eyes, saying, "Emily, pretend you're somewhere else. You're on a beach! You're on Sanibel Island. We're walking there right now!" I could only look angrily as the pain continued. Finally, a baby needle was miraculously brought out and a vein in my hand decided to cooperate. Fast-forward back to 2014.

As soon as I heard the words "blood work" escape my doctor's mouth, I couldn't help but re-live the nightmare I described above. And believe me, that's not a pleasant stroll down memory lane. It's more like a sprint through a horrific back alley! My body tensed as I mentally made note of everything I needed to take care of. Pick up my medication at the pharmacy. Check. Get x-rays done. Check. Buy a ton of cranberry juice. Check. Ask my Dad how to survive kidney stones. Check, check, check. Get blood work taken care of. I didn't want to say check.

But this was something I had to do.

So early the next day, my roommate and I made the trek back to the doctor's office for my dreaded blood work. I was nervous. My palms were sweating. I wanted to cry. All I could envision was the nurse hanging me upside-down and drawing blood from my neck. The fear was real. I wanted to escape. And then my name was called. The moment had come. I walked back and took a seat.

As the typical "find a vein" search started, I stared fearfully at my roommate and asked her to hold my hand. She tried to take my mind off of it as the nurse said, "Here we go." And it just happened. I felt a tiny prick. But it happened. There was no pain, no second tries, no hanging me upside down. It worked. I stared fear in the face and won. And after winning, I celebrated with a smoothie and the reminder to "squeeze" the day. It only seemed fitting.

The night before that appointment, I was on the phone with my parents, talking through the events of the week, when my Dad said something that really resonated with me: "Emily, you're not in the same condition you were in back in 2009. You're in a different place. You were dehydrated when they couldn't find your veins. Now, you're not."

This may seem obvious, but to me, a light bulb went off. There is pain, grief, shame and sorrow in my past that I don't want to revisit. There are moments in life when I felt like I was hung upside-down, screaming in pain, angry at myself or the decisions of those around me. Sometimes thinking back to those situations, people, and places makes me feel the pain all over again. I don't want to look at the dehydrated moments of my life. I want to run away, full-steam ahead.

But we must face our fear, our pain, and our shame, and choose to conquer it in order to move forward. Here's what I learned: I was in a different place emotionally, spiritually, physically and mentally in the moments of my past that bring me pain. The decisions I made then stem from a dehydrated heart, a heart not choosing to be the woman God made me to be.

Shame isn't a flighty emotion of regret I feel after devouring an entire case of Double Stuf Oreos singlehandedly. Shame goes so much deeper than a sugar rush. Shame bleeds deep down into my core, into the places no one sees. Shame threatens to haunt me.

Here's what I must establish every day: will shame define me or refine me? I get to choose whether I will be the hero, victim, or villain in my story. We all fail, we all mess up—it's a part of being human. Mistakes are normal and it's healthy to mourn decisions, but how can we move forward? How can we choose to not live in the decisions of yesterday?

I remember sitting with my Mom several years ago on my journey, broken over a decision I had made. With tear-filled eyes, I looked at her and asked, "How could Jesus not be ashamed of me when I am so ashamed of myself?" Without hesitating, she replied, "Emily, where in the Bible does it say God is ashamed of you?" Nowhere. Not in one single place. In fact, on every page I turn in God's Word, I find Jesus conquering shame and whispering into the deepest crevices of my heart, "Emily, I know you and I love you. I see your sin and I love you anyway."

Nothing in our story takes God by surprise. He knows us and He loves us.

> You saw me before I was born. Every day of my life was recorded in your book. Every moment was laid out before a single day had passed.
>
> (Psalm 139:16, NLT)

When Jesus was nailed to the cross, He took each and every one of my sins with Him. He sacrificed Himself and He scorned shame because He loved me that much (Hebrews 12:2). He left Heaven for Earth to pick me up, brush the dirt off my face and say, "Baby girl, your sins are forgiven. I have wiped you clean. You are whole and you don't have to live in this shame. I love you that much."

Perhaps the biggest hindrance to finally overcoming shame is that we haven't fully embraced what Jesus already did for us. If we hold onto our shame, what did Jesus die for? When I choose to grip my shame with clenched fists, I'm essentially looking at Jesus and saying, "What you did for me wasn't enough." The thought of that breaks my heart. And yet that's what I've been doing, that's where I've been living.

I don't have a fancy checklist or easy 5-step plan for overcoming shame. It's a battle, but warrior friends, it's already been won on the cross. So, what's helping me with my struggle with shame?

Admitting my sin and turning from it. Let's not stand in the way of our own healing by holding our shame inside. Who are your people? The first, and one of the most important steps I've taken on this journey, is admitting where I've messed up to those I trust. To move forward, we must walk in the same grace we preach.

> You can't whitewash your sins and get by with it; you find mercy by admitting and leaving them.
> (Proverbs 28:13, MSG)

Live freely. After admitting my mess-ups, I've asked those I trust to hold me accountable, and I'm choosing to not give sin the time of day, completely cutting out anything that takes me back to my places of shame. Perhaps it's a relationship, maybe it's a specific location, or a song, or a movie. Identify those people, places and things and draw a line in the sand.

> Could it be any clearer? Our old way of life was nailed to the cross with Christ, a decisive end to that sin-miserable life—no longer at sin's every beck and call! What we believe is this: If we get included in Christ's sin-conquering death, we also get included in his life-saving resurrection. We know that when Jesus was raised from the dead it was a signal of the end of death-as-the-end. Never again will death have the last word. When Jesus died, he took sin down with him, but alive he brings God down to us. From now on, think of it this way: Sin speaks a dead language that means nothing to you; God speaks your mother tongue, and you hang on every word. You are dead to sin and alive to God. That's what Jesus did. That means you must not give sin a vote in the way you conduct your lives. Don't give it the time of day. Don't even run little errands that are connected with that old way of life. Throw yourselves wholeheartedly and full-time—remember, you've been raised from the dead!—into God's way of doing things. Sin can't tell you how to live. After all, you're not living under that old tyranny any longer. You're living in the freedom of God. (Romans 6:6-14, MSG)

Embrace healing in the name of Jesus. Remember our friend in John 4, the Samaritan woman at the well? She discovered freedom and victory from shame when she ran back to her town speaking His name. We stamp victory on shame when we apply Jesus' name.

> But now that you've found you don't have to listen to sin tell you what to do, and have discovered the delight of listening to God telling you, what a surprise! A whole, healed, put-together life right now, with more and more of life on the way! Work hard for sin your whole life and your pension is death. But God's gift is real life, eternal life, delivered by Jesus, our Master.
>
> (Romans 6:22-23, MSG)

Warrior friend, let's just close the chapters we've been trying so desperately to hide, forget, and scrub clean from our lives. It's time to lace up our boots and fight for victory. He knows us. He loves us.

And He's already won for us. We are free.

We find healing from our past hurts, habits and hang-ups by nourishing our souls—replenishing that which was dead with the life-giving water of Jesus. I'm not that same broken-down girl who made the decisions I was ashamed of anymore. I'm forgiven. I'm free. I'm redeemed. And I am whole.

That being said, I don't have to be terrified looking at my past. I don't need to be nervous, scared, or ashamed when I walk into a place that reminds me of past decisions, or see an individual that makes me think of past hurt. I can stare at my pain and conquer it because I'm not that girl anymore. I'm changing, growing, healing, and becoming who God made me to be.

Sometimes we just have to stare at our pain head-on in order to discover healing and breakthrough. And please hear me: I'm not saying to be unwise here. It would be foolish to deliberately walk into unsafe, unhealthy situations that could cause harm or stunt the growth God is doing in us. I'm talking about situations and circumstances outside our control: memories, flashbacks, people, and the healing process itself. Healing takes time. It takes a whole lot of prayer. And it takes the courage to face your fears.

I'm thankful I'm not the same girl from 2009 who was so dehydrated that it took 16 tries before the 17th IV needle stuck. I'm thankful I was able to look fear in the face and have blood work done without being hung upside-down. I'm thankful I'm not the same girl who made those mistakes she wishes she could forget. I'm coming to a place where I actually believe it's okay to not be okay. And it's okay to make mistakes. Perhaps my biggest mistakes and some of my deepest pain will be what I can use to help people the most. If anything, that pain has helped me discover more of who Emily is—and isn't—than ever before. As a result, I've learned more about God's grace in a way I never imagined, and I'm finally beginning to believe that shame doesn't define me. The internal battles and fearful wars can end because I'm not the same girl anymore. I'm the girl who can stare fear in the face and win.

hope and healing in addiction.

"Though no one can go back and make a brand new start, anyone can start from now and make a brand new ending."

- Carl Bard

Just from hearing my Dad's voice on the phone, I immediately knew something was wrong. As he shared that my cousin overdosed from a bad batch of fentanyl and died the night before, my mind froze in shock.

Brittany was only 24, two months away from her 25th birthday. She was born in August of 1991—right after me and our cousin, Ashley, that May and June. We were so close in age, I remember summer camps together, giggling, sharing secrets, Christmas celebrations opening presents and singing songs, and endless dance parties.

How could someone I love, someone so young, with all the potential in the world, in the blink of an eye just be gone? My heart broke as I began sobbing, grieving the life of my cousin, my family, cut too short.

The more I think of Brittany, the more I can't help but see

her gorgeous smile, freely laughing, finding the joy in life. And yet, along the way, the pain of life seeped its way into her heart, whispering the lie that she could find something to numb what she was feeling—even if for just a little while.

We all experience pain and we all numb our hurts differently. For some of us it's devouring a carton of ice cream. For others, it's spending countless hours at the gym, running from boyfriend to boyfriend, self harming, consuming everything in sight and purging later (or not eating at all), gossiping, maxing out our credit cards, obsessing over cleaning the house until spotless, planning on one glass of wine at dinner only to drink the entire bottle, Netflix binging, pornography, and the list goes on.

Numbing our pain is just that—numbing it. Sure we'll feel good for a little while, but eventually our temporary fix wears off, leaving us more depleted, more empty than before, ready to chase our next high. Addiction is addiction—whether it's drugs and alcohol or Pinterest obsession. One addiction is not "greater" or "worse" than another. We all have hang ups, we all have hurts, we all have bruises. Life hurts, and it's hard. But I believe that even in the darkest storms in our lives, there is hope. I'm banking my life on that. Believing that God sent His one and only Son to die for me is a game changer in my story. Even on my darkest days, when I want to turn to my vices to numb the pain away, I know my story's not over yet and I'm going to be okay because I'm banking everything on the hope I have in Jesus Christ.

Pain is real. I know what you're going through is real and hard and there are days it seems impossible to put one foot in front of the other. I know it's tempting to numb what you're feeling with a temporary fix. I've been there, fighting the urge to numb my pain away. Warrior friend, don't give up. Don't allow the darkness to overcome your smile. Grip tightly the hope we have in Christ with everything you've got and don't let go.

Here are a few next best steps in standing rooted on the hope we have in Christ and finding freedom from addiction:

Get honest with yourself. Don't try to sweep your addiction under the rug pretending it's not there. What pain are you trying to numb? How are you numbing it? One of the most freeing things we can do is be honest with ourselves.

Talk with God. God knows you—He created you! Talk with Him about your pain, what you're experiencing, what you're angry about, and your disappointments. If you've never begun a relationship with Jesus, today's the day! Simply ask Him to be your Lord and Savior, to forgive you, and guide you with each next step. God can handle you being angry at Him or unsure about Him. Just start talking!

Talk with someone you trust today. We weren't created to do life alone; God designed us to do life together. Talk with someone you trust and share with them what's going on and how you're numbing your pain. Ask them to hold you accountable and walk with you as you grip onto hope and let go of addiction.

Talk with a Christian counselor. Counseling isn't bad, something to shy away from or be ashamed of. Ask your church for recommended Christian counselors in your area and make an appointment.

Journal. Write out your emotions, what you're thinking, how you're feeling. Ask yourself questions, jot down observations, document your journey.

Define a clear next step. What's your next step in becoming free from addiction? If you're not sure, talk with your mentor or counselor and define a game plan to break free.

As I celebrate Brittany's life and grieve over her story ending too soon, I'm filled with renewed courage to face my hurt and pain and not try to stuff it down or numb it away. I don't want my pain to swallow me—our pain and hurt doesn't define us. God defines us and He says we are loved, called, made with purpose, worthy, beautiful and enough. Warrior friend, we're becoming. We're going to have hurt and heartache on the journey, but there is incredible hope in Jesus Christ.

Brittany, I love you. I am so happy you're now pain free in the arms of our Heavenly Father. I'm excited to see you again. Much love.

what do you need to leave behind?

"It's no use going back to yesterday, because I was a different person then."

- Lewis Carroll

In December 2015, I was preparing to make my second cross country move from the fabulous city of Las Vegas back to sunny Florida. As I made my game plan, I knew I didn't want to make the 2,233-mile trek with a trailer in tow, so I began sifting through my apartment (a.k.a. the #babecave), making piles "to keep," "to throw away," "to give away," and so on.

I thought I had sorted through everything really well, and as the eve of my moving date arrived, I was even patting myself on the back for a job well done in prioritizing what to keep and leave behind.

And then I tried to put everything in my little red convertible...

Let's just say, not everything fit. I thought I had gone through my stuff. I thought I had truly whittled down to only what I needed, but I was still left with piles left over. Rather than taking the time to go through the overflowing bags again, I decided to ship what wouldn't fit in my car. Win-win... or so I thought.

My Mom and I piled my car with bags, drove to FedEx, and stuffed boxes with clothes and pillows to send across the country. I paid the shipping and moved on, not thinking twice about it—until about three weeks later in Florida when I unpacked, cleaned out my closet, and then proceeded to get rid of the same amount of items I had just paid to ship across country.

Face palm

I paid to ship stuff that a few weeks later I ended up getting rid of. I could have used the baggage fees to buy new clothes, rather than worrying about shipping the old!

Isn't this so like life? Stepping into a new season, a new chapter, a new day, a new year, I tend to want to cram all of the old in with the new, not realizing that in doing so, I'm paying a baggage fee.

When I carry unforgiveness with me, I'm paying in broken relationships and internal chaos.

When I carry anger with me, I'm paying in missed moments.

When I carry others' expectations with me, I'm paying by exchanging freedom for straight up bondage.

When I carry fear with me, I'm paying by missing out on what I was made to do, to be.

When I carry the pursuit of perfection with me, I'm paying in insecurity in who I am and who I'm becoming.

When we don't take the time to sort through the present and the past keeping only what's valuable or useful, we ultimately can't make room for the new. We pay for everything we carry—but not all baggage fees are bad. When I set my alarm for an early morning workout, I'm paying in the form of an hour less of sleep under warm, cozy covers! But I'm gaining health and strong muscles.

> This is what God says, the God who builds a road right through the ocean, who carves a path through pounding waves, the God who summons horses and chariots and armies—they lie down and then can't get up; they're snuffed out like so many candles: "Forget about what's happened; don't keep going over old history. Be alert, be present. I'm about to do something brand-new. It's bursting out! Don't you see it? There it is! I'm making a road through the desert, rivers in the badlands."
>
> (Isaiah 43:16-19, MSG)

In order to become who God made you to be, you just have to choose to be you. And to choose to be you, you've got to decide what you're going to carry with you... and what you're going to pay for it with.

There are many things I want to carry with me into the next chapter of my becoming story:

Love
Laughter
Friendship
Lacing up my warrior boots
Growing stronger
Learning new things
Embracing the journey, the process, the becoming.

As I'm reflecting on previous seasons and stepping into the

new, I've also assessed bags I don't want to ship into the future, I don't want to pay for them, I want to leave them behind:

Unforgiveness
The pursuit for perfection
Shame
Fear of failure
Fear of missing out
Doubting that God does know what He's doing
Being so hard on myself.

We've all got suitcases we carry headed into the next chapter of becoming. What do you want to carry with you? What do you want to leave behind?

If I could rewind time and go back to my little piles in the #babecave, I would have said, "Emily, you don't need this stuff... you're going to get rid of it anyway! Don't pay the couple hundred dollars to ship it. Leave it behind." In 365 days, I don't want to look back on kicking off a new chapter with the same feeling, wishing I would have left things behind.

Warrior friend, let's do the heavy lifting today. It's worth it tomorrow. And the next day and the next. What do you need to leave behind?

why i didn't think i was beautiful, until i did.

"She remembered who she was and the game changed."
- Anonymous

"Are you headed back to school?"

Sigh. If only I could count how many times I've been asked that question in airport terminals.

No. I am no longer a freshman in high school. I am in fact a twenty-something. I have a full time job. I own a car. I'm saving for retirement. I am an adult. With a major case of baby face.

Growing up, I always felt slightly awkward. Tall. Gangly. Braces. Even, *ahem*, head gear at one point. The typical spout of acne. I never knew what to do with my hair. And make-up? I couldn't even tell you where to start.

Once I hit my freshman year of college, I felt like I finally started growing into myself. Maybe I'm what you'd classify as a late bloomer. Growing up, I struggled with an extreme underbite requiring surgery to correct the bone structure of my jaw. Due to bone development, I wasn't able to undergo surgery until I was "officially" done growing. So, when my freshman year of college arrived and I was rolled into the operating room, I couldn't help but be excited—I was about to have one of my more visible insecurities corrected.

The surgery ended up being more complicated than anticipated, and I had to undergo a series of smaller surgeries over the course of the next five years to finish what the doctors started. But by the time it was all said and done, my smile was fixed. I would no longer suffer from the jaw problems I had been experiencing and would be able to flash my pearly whites with confidence. This was my moment. *I would now be beautiful.*

But you know what? I was still the same me. The same Emily still resided in my skin. And restructuring my face didn't change that. While I assumed I'd conquered insecurity with a jaw procedure, I vastly underestimated the power my mind had on my beauty all along. Having a new, improved smile didn't boost my confidence in a way that lasted. It just shifted my focus onto other areas—what about my skin? What about my hair? And why couldn't I figure out how to use make-up?!

Do you ever catch yourself looking in the mirror dissatisfied with what you're seeing? Hair just not working right. Not the right shade of lip stick. A few more pimples than you wanted. Eyebrows not *on fleek*. Morning routines are a struggle. And the more I cake on, the less confident I feel.

But the underlying pressure is there. The other girls I interact with seem to have it figured out. Their hair looks silky smooth and styled just right. They know what to do with beauty supplies. Acne? They don't have that! And goodness, those eyebrows. They are on point! From the pictures in magazines, the perfectly posed selfies on Instagram, and seemingly perfect models on the latest Bachelor season, it seems like I just can't keep up. And then I'm asked if I'm a high school student.

Can I sigh again?

While the struggle and pressure and unspoken demand for

perfection is there, I've come to discover that whatever I do on the outside can't really fix the way I see the outside. Just like I control the temperature in my home by the thermostat on the wall, I control my beauty by the thermostat of my mind. When I discovered this, I saw for the first time that I am already beautiful—I don't have to try so hard. I am made in the image of God (Genesis 1:27); He designed me uniquely & wonderfully (Psalm 139); and He says I am a masterpiece (Ephesians 2:10).

When I'm unsure of my hair, my make-up, and my smile, I project that image to those around me. My shoulders slump. The bounce in my step is missing. And there certainly isn't a glimmer in my eye. However, when I push my shoulders back and hold my head high, choosing to smile even if I have no clue what it means to "contour," I exude beauty.

"Charm is deceptive, and beauty does not last; but a woman who fears the Lord will be greatly praised." (Proverbs 31:30, NIV)

I've heard the same cliches you have, but you know what, some of them are actually true. The best make-up is a smile. The girls who choose joy are the prettiest. Don't believe me? Just look up. Look at the girls around you. Do your own secret investigative work. Observe the girls in your circle. What defines the beauty you see? What catches your eye first? Now look again. Look past the make-up and make-up free faces and into her eyes. Look at how she's carrying herself. Does she seem content? Full of joy? Satisfied? What we see initially in the mirror isn't what defines us. It's what we see the second time that does. It's what's lying directly underneath the surface that matters. We are beautiful because we believe we are, because we were created in beauty, because we are daughters of the King.

"As a face is reflected in water, so the heart reflects the real person." (Proverbs 27:19, NLT)

Warrior friend, you are beautiful.

You are already enough.

You are the definition of drop-dead gorgeous.

You just need to see it first and then choose to share the gift of YOU with the rest of us.

What do you see when you look in the mirror? Take a second look. What do you see just beyond the surface. You. Are. Beautiful.

the day God hugged me in the starbucks drive-through line.

"I lift up my eyes to the mountains—where does my help come from? My help comes from the Lord, the Maker of heaven and earth. He will not let your foot slip—he who watches over you will not slumber; indeed, he who watches over Israel will neither slumber nor sleep.

The Lord watches over you—the Lord is your shade at your right hand; the sun will not harm you by day, nor the moon by night. The Lord will keep you from all harm—he will watch over your life; the Lord will watch over your coming and going both now and forevermore."

- Psalm 121, NIV

In December 2015, I had a realization in the Starbucks drive-through that made me want to cry. It was a typical Monday. I was running errands, wrapping up projects at work and needing just one more cup of coffee. Completely normal, completely typical. And the coffee struggle was very, very real.

I remember debating whether I should run home to brew a fresh pot of coffee or swing through the closest Starbucks drive-through for a refreshing iced coffee with caramel sweetener and soy milk. In the moment, the choice seemed obvious. Starbucks it was.

As I drove, I dove headfirst into a nostalgic moment. My mind was running through the series of checklists I needed to conquer before hopping on an airplane to head home for Christmas. And suddenly it hit me like a ton of bricks: ***I was about to get on an airplane to go home for Christmas.***

This may seem trivial, but that was the first time I had ever done this—the first time I hadn't been home for all of the pre-holiday festivities like baking cookies, decorating the house, attending parties and Christmas productions. I was on the opposite side of the country from my family jamming to "I'll Be Home For Christmas" suddenly realizing those lyrics fit the tune of my life. And that realization made me want to cry.

My tears weren't tears of sadness or depression, just tears of realization. And tears of feeling by myself far away from those closest to me. Tears of understanding, tears of joy, tears of excitement. Tears of wrapping up a year of many firsts, new adventures, lots of growth, and lots of becoming more of the Emily God made me to be.

In that moment, I just wanted a hug. I wanted to feel that someone was with me and that the 2,000 miles separating me from my family wasn't that big. The excitement of the family I had established in Nevada and how soon I would be reunited with my family in Florida were colliding and my heart was bursting at the seams. I felt the immensity of the love and community I experienced, but wanted to not be holding that alone.

I ordered my venti iced coffee in the drive-through and turned up my radio while I waited for my turn to pay and be on my way. As I pulled up to the cashier's window, I grabbed my phone, ready to whip out my Starbucks app, when the barista looked at me with a sparkle in her eyes and said, "The car in front of you bought your coffee today. Merry Christmas!" Stunned, I thanked her profusely, accepted the caffeinated gift and drove away before she could see me burst into tears.

God reached down and hugged me in the drive-through through a complete stranger that day. He reminded me that I'm not alone by gifting me a simple cup of coffee.

As I drove away, I knew I had accepted a divine appointment when I made the decision to swing through Starbucks rather than rush home. And I was so thankful that the person in front of me listened to a simple nudge to pay for coffee for the person behind them. That simple gesture of kindness from someone I don't know spoke into the depths of my heart so deeply, so profoundly, so personally.

In that drive-through with that cup of coffee, Jesus reminded me, "Emily, you're not alone here. Distance doesn't separate family. Family is around you. Family is in you. I am here. I am with you. You are not alone here."

I am not alone here.

And like a tidal wave, instances, moments and memories began rushing to the forefront of my mind of how so many people—people who at one point were complete strangers to me—embraced me, adopting me as their own. In those moments and places when I feel alone, the reality is, I'm not. I'm surrounded by people who love me—people in Nevada and people who, in that moment, were 2,000 miles away in Florida. It doesn't matter where you're located geographically for you to show love to someone. Love is something we express, something we say, something we feel, something we live. Love is who we choose to be. And there's no room for isolation in love.

In the moments I feel alone, I'm going to remind myself of a stranger who bought me a cup of coffee and the sweet whisper from my Savior reminding the depths of my soul, "You're not alone here."

Warrior friend, neither are you. You're not alone here. One of my favorite sayings I hear my Daddy share over and over? When your hope is rooted in Christ, He is WITH you, He is IN you, and He is FOR you. He truly, truly is.

I am beautiful.

I am loved.

I am enough.

the real story behind galentine's day.

"Real queens fix each other's crowns."

- Anonymous

I didn't say anything profound to the warrior women staring back at me—in fact, I said something really simple: "You are beautiful and you are loved. Just because you don't have a dude making dinner reservations for you tonight doesn't mean you're less of a person. You are enough. And someday I'll be celebrating with you and crying at your wedding."

Let's rewind a few weeks, shall we? About two weeks before the ever-so-popular #SinglesAwarenessDay, my heart began aching for the precious women around me. Conversations were bubbling to the surface centered around dinner reservations, crushes, favorite flowers, hopes, and another round of crushed dreams. I just couldn't take it.

In years past, Valentine's Day was hit or miss for me. Sometimes I didn't care, and at other times it irritated me that I wasn't a part of the candy hearts club. I mean, who doesn't want Prince Charming riding in and sweeping you off your feet into the sunset?

But this year was different. February 14th was hitting me in a way it never had before—I was seeing it through the eyes of so many of my warrior friends. And I found myself staring at a beautiful, talented, sassy and classy group of women who felt like they just didn't measure up.

And that realization broke me.

As I chatted with my friends one thought resounded in my brain like bricks in a dryer: *why not create an intentional environment to celebrate the women in my life and this stage of life we're in?*

Hello, Galentine's Day.

I whipped up a cute little invite, texted my single ladies, and started pinning the craftiest Galentine's ideas out there to my Pinterest board. The weeks marched on until it was finally Saturday night and I just couldn't wait for my gals to come over.

One by one, they arrived. We hugged. We laughed. We ate chocolate until we couldn't eat any more. We dreamed. We asked questions. And then I said that very simple statement I opened with:

"You are beautiful and you are loved. Just because you don't have a dude making dinner reservations for you tonight doesn't mean you're less of a person. You are enough. And someday I'll be celebrating with you and crying at your wedding."

Those words had been burning in my heart the entire day leading up to my first time hosting a "Galentine's Day" party. And as I said them, I knew it was important that I didn't leave them unsaid. Tears welled up across the room. We cried and we laughed. We dreamed of fairy tales to come. And as we did, I prayed. I prayed and I thanked Jesus for this journey of becoming. I thanked Him that on a night where so many focus on dinner dates and roses, I was able to look into the eyes of eight precious women and remind them "you are enough." And in reminding them, I reminded myself of this same truth, too.

God's nudging isn't random. It's a constant reminder to be the people He says we are—to be who He created us to be. My heart broke at the thought that women might feel less valued, less cherished and less loved on a single day of the year simply because they don't have a date. And out of that brokenness a fun, new tradition was born.

Ladies (and guys too!), February 14th shouldn't diminish who you are as a person. You don't need romantic dinner reservations to be deemed worthy or valuable. You already are. You are beautiful. You are cherished. You are loved. You are worthy. God sent His only Son to die for you because He loves you that much. And He didn't require a dozen roses as a prerequisite for His love. He loves you for you. And that is enough.

No matter what day of the year it is, never lose sight of your worth. You are a daughter of the King. And you are oh-so-worthy.

6:00 a.m. friends.

"Your life is a direct reflection of how you think."
- Mark Cummins

I can count on one hand the number of people I could call at 6:00 a.m. who would answer the phone. These individuals—some by blood, others by mutual life experiences—would move heaven and earth to help me if I asked. I don't have to beg or plead for their help. They just help me.

I've never thought of God as a 6:00 a.m. friend until recently. On the verge of making an important decision, I was asked if I had talked to God about it. I looked at my friend hesitantly, knowing they were expecting the truth, but not wanting to admit that I hadn't. I assumed that this opportunity had come straight from God and I didn't need to give it a second thought. But that question pricked my heart in a way I wasn't expecting.

Had I talked to God about it? What was I supposed to do? I couldn't wait on making my decision for some bold sign in the sky or audible voice, and frankly, I had no clue how I would even know what God was trying to say to me. Would I hear a "yes" or "no," or just feel a certain feeling, signaling which path I should take? I wrestled within myself. I searched my Bible for a verse that would make me feel warm and fuzzy. I frantically sought a sensation of peace so that I could pillow my head that night with direction and purpose.

None of that came.

It wasn't until my eyelids were heavy and the hour hand on my clock ticked later and later into the night that I began to hear something. In all of my dizzying rush to force an answer out of God, I hadn't been listening at all. I had just been knocking on the door, not pausing to give Him the opportunity to actually open it up. In the stillness of my room, I never received that audibly loud, booming God-voice or visit from an angel, but I did receive a "peace that passes all understanding," (Philippians 4:7). I had knocked, or perhaps more accurately, banged on the door, and God answered.

> "Then he said to them, 'Suppose one of you has a friend, and he goes to him at midnight and says, Friend, lend me three loaves of bread, because a friend of mine on a journey has come to me, and I have nothing to set before him. Then the one inside answers, 'Don't bother me. The door is already locked, and my children are with me in bed. I can't get up and give you anything.' I tell you, though he will not get up and give him the bread because he is his friend, yet because of the man's boldness he will get up and give him as much as he needs.'" (Luke 11:5-8, NIV)

I think talking to God is a lot like the picture Luke gives us in the parable of the two friends. There was a camaraderie rooted deep inside this friendship, a confidence that they would have each other's back—even if it meant getting out of bed in the middle of the night. All they had to do was knock and they'd receive an answer.

I bang on God's door too much. I do all the talking and asking, and rarely stop knocking. I don't take my fist away from the door long enough to give room for God to open it up to me. Perhaps the root of the issue is that I don't trust that He will, in fact, open the door. When a situation calls for action, I want to grab life with both hands and make it happen. I think God will be too busy to get out of bed, and offer me His bread. So I create my own pseudo-bread made of my own ideas and actions. And each time I do this, I'm not satisfied, and the bread, well, it just doesn't taste like bread.

Maybe this story is more about faith than it is about bread or travelers or waking someone up in the middle of the night. Maybe it's a story about trusting in a God who is eager to respond to my knocking.

I don't question the reliability of my 6:00 a.m. friends at all. In fact, I have complete confidence that they would help me without a second thought. I want to see God that way too. I want to live freely in the assurance that He won't leave me standing in the cold, pounding on His front door. I want to embrace a God who is good and who can be trusted.

Now when I talk to God, I'm not approaching a door doubting that I'll be invited inside. I'm approaching a door knowing that all I have to do is knock and He'll open it wide, fresh baked bread waiting.

becoming katie.

This chapter was written by a fellow warrior with you in mind.

Becoming Katie… wow, that has been and still is a journey. What I have learned lately is that it needs to start with loving myself the way God loves me!

I'm learning that loving myself starts in my mind! I have struggled my whole life with comparison and believing that I'm not good enough. I had this belief in my mind that if I didn't win or wasn't the best, then it wasn't worth finishing, or in some cases even trying! When I was younger and my family would be on vacation, my sister and I used to race down the beach. We would always pick a starting line and would race back towards our parents (a.k.a. the finish line). My little legs would start out strong, but anytime I saw my sister start to pull ahead and I knew she was going to win, I would stop racing. I let my mind believe that if I pulled up and stopped running, then she didn't really win—I let her win. Not trying or finishing felt safer than giving my best and still failing or still falling short.

This was the mindset I was living in, but I wasn't happy. I grew tired of overthinking everything, tired of fear sitting in my driver's seat, and tired of not believing in myself. Something needed to change. This is where loving myself the way God loves me comes in.

When my Mom was pregnant with me, my parents had to go through routine tests during the pregnancy. One of those tests came back negative, and the doctor shared that my brain and spinal cord were not properly developing at that stage in the pregnancy. Their doctor recommended terminating the pregnancy. My parents believed and knew that God had a plan and purpose for my life and I am sitting here today sharing my story with you because of their decision to not terminate the pregnancy!

From the beginning, God has had a plan for me. But when I let fear and doubt drive my view of myself, I can't walk out in God's plan. This is when I knew my mindset needed to change. I needed to turn down the soundtrack on the lies I had told myself for so long.

Lie #1: If I fail at something, then I am wrong or bad.

Truth #1: If I fail at something and I know that I gave my best effort, I am strong and courageous for trying something new and then choosing to learn and grow for the next thing!

Lie #2: I am not good enough.

Truth #2: I am a daughter of God and He formed me in my Mother's womb for such a time as this. He has equipped and qualified me for His plan and purpose.

Lie #3: I can't do anything right.

Truth #3: God has given me wisdom and discernment to make decisions and I can trust myself.

Loving myself is a battle every day. Responding to lies with truth is one way I fight the battle.

Another way I fight the battle is by getting to know myself and doing the inner work to grow. I have used the Enneagram as a tool to dig into my motivation and core fears and have even had sessions with an Enneagram Coach who guided me through the journey. I also lined my bathroom mirror with flashcards filled with Scriptures, prayers, and truth I choose to speak over myself.

And I am working on finding the right routine that helps me win each day. I used to see other's workout or morning routines and I would think, "Wow, they are so disciplined and successful, I should do what they are doing." But I either wouldn't ever start, or I would try for a day or two and then move on to something else. But I would beat myself up in my mind, saying things like, "You can't do anything. You can't commit to or finish anything." That is when my Dad encouraged me to start small with one step each day and to find the routine, the workouts that fuel me and that I enjoy, and then if you miss a day extend yourself grace and say, "Ok, let's try again tomorrow."

So that is what I have been doing... one day, one step at a time working towards goals and dreams that I had been burying because I was too afraid to try.

This is... *becoming me.*

warrior steps.

Hey warrior friend, at the end of each section in this book, you'll find "warrior steps" simply designed for you to, reflect and talk to God about your becoming story. My prayer is that this space becomes a launching pad for your journey choosing to be who God made you to be!

Mark up these pages or grab a journal and spend time dreaming, praying... becoming you!

(1) What is your water jar you need to give to God, trusting Him to do what only He can do in your life?

(2) Discouraging days will come. The question is, how will we lace up our warrior boots & choose to respond? Write Psalm 42:5 on a sticky note to put somewhere you'll see it often, serving as a reminder of Who to look to & trust.

(3) What step(s) do you need to take today to overcome shame?

(4) Are you struggling to find freedom? What steps will you take today to walk freely on your becoming journey?

(5) What do you want to carry with you on your becoming journey? Make a list identifying the characteristics you want to live out moving forward... and then, make a list of all the things you want to leave behind. Put your lists somewhere you can see them often, reminding you of who you want to be.

(6) Do you struggle with how you view yourself? Spend time reading Genesis 1:27, Psalm 139, Ephesians 2:10, Proverbs 31:30, and Proverbs 27:19. Ask God to help you see and believe how He sees you.

(7) Reflect on a time in your story you felt God comfort you in an unexpected way (like in the Starbucks drive through line)? Spend time thanking God for the hope we have in Him!

(8) Whether it's February 14th or not, mark a time on your calendar to gather your friends and remind them of how incredible they are... in doing so, you'll be encouraged too, warrior friend.

(9) Spend time talking with God today... Journal your prayer, go for a walk and talk... Spend time in His presence! He wants to talk with you!

choose to be her.

"You know who you want to be. You just have to choose to be her."
- Mark Cummins

who do you want to be?

"What is really hard, and really amazing, is giving up on being perfect and beginning the work of becoming yourself."
- Mark Cummins

I vividly remember finding myself head-first in a collision with depression in the summer of 2016. I felt stuck, numb, trapped. And I didn't know what to do.

More accurately, I didn't know who I wanted to be.

In the course of a few short months, I had embraced risk and change and adventure with both hands making my second cross-country move to launch a business, and after the adrenaline wore off, I was left with the crushing pressure of next...

What client would I sign with *next*?
What speaking gig would I book *next*?
What would BecomingMe.TV do *next*?

As I listened to the voices and ideas and excitement circling around me, I was excited, too. I hustled and worked my heart out, but collapsed exhausted in my parents' living room six months into my entrepreneurial stint, feeling too empty to cry.

It was here, in the unknown, that I was reminded that I do know, I've always known, who I wanted to be. In my fear of failure, my Dad looked me straight in the eyes and said a statement I haven't let out of my sight since: "Emily, you know who you want to be. You just have to choose to be her."

In that moment, the fog lifted. The lightbulb in my head flashed on, and I unlocked the bars to the prison I had trapped myself in. The pressure and ideas and questions and next, next, next swirling around me? It was there and it was real. But it only consumed me because I allowed it to. I gave the external pressure permission to begin defining my life, my story, who I'm becoming, and it left me standing empty-handed in the middle of a prison cell. The funny thing is, I had the key to set myself free all along: the freedom to choose.

Deep down, we know who we want to be. I'm not talking "do" here. I'm talking "be." Please don't miss the difference. I haven't always known what I wanted to *do*—career, school choices, what car to buy, where to eat for lunch—but I have intrinsically known who I want to *be*: a woman who loves Jesus, daily ditches the pursuit of perfection, relentlessly pursues becoming who God has made me to be, and helps as many people as I can become who God made them to be, too. That's it. How that's carried out changes as I grow... the methods change, but the *who*, the *why*, doesn't.

Far too often, we allow other voices, circumstances, expectations, challenges, and life to dictate who we are, what we should do, who we should be, and who we should become. But here's the thing: no one else—no circumstance or person—has the power to be you. Only you have the power to choose to be who God made you to be. You can choose to be who everyone else tells you to be, or you can choose to be who you know you want to be and who God made you to be all along.

I love the scene in the 2017 movie *Wonder Woman* when Diana sees the challenge and opportunity before her in "No Man's Land." Sensing her frustration and determination to cross the land no man has dared to travel, Steve, her friend and closest companion on the journey, discourages her from the mission—even stating that's not what they came to do. Diana found herself at her own intersection. Would she lean into what those around her were telling her to do and to be? Or would she choose to be herself?

What's the "No Man's Land" in front of you? As I sat in my parent's living room talking with my Dad that summer, my No Man's Land looked like shutting down the business I started and stepping into a full time role on a church team I love. That was one of the best decisions I've ever made. Looking back through each of the chapters in my becoming story, I never regret the moments I stepped out, trusting God, choosing to be me.

Maybe your No Man's Land looks like making a phone call and asking someone you've hurt for forgiveness; maybe it's stepping out of an unhealthy relationship; perhaps it's enrolling in classes at your local college and pursuing the next level of your education; maybe it looks like sending your resume and applying for that job; perhaps it means having that doctor's exam you've been putting off because you're nervous about what the results may be; maybe it's renewing your membership at the gym, setting your alarm clock earlier and exercising; perhaps it's initiating new friendships and inviting people to dinner; maybe it's writing a book, painting that masterpiece, or designing that piece of art you've always dreamt of; perhaps it means going through the steps to become a foster parent; maybe it looks like going on a missions trip; maybe it looks like serving at your local church; perhaps it looks like inviting that friend to have coffee and telling her about Jesus.

What's the thing that wakes you up in the middle of the night? What makes you cry? What breaks your heart and brings you the most joy? Friend, that's your THING, that's your WHY, that's the indicator of the No Man's Land you must cross.

My primary "whys" have been in my heart since I was a little girl—writing, empowering people, and investing my life in ministry. This was the No Man's Land I needed to conquer that summer...

I closed the chapter of a business endeavor that wasn't made for me and stepped back into vocational ministry in a local church and continued to partner with people through BecomingMe.TV. I chose to be her and stepped out.

You have this power, too. How can you fight to become who God made you to be? Choose to be her. Choose to be her right now, again in five minutes, later today, tomorrow, the day after, and the day after that... every minute you choose to be her, you're fighting to become who God made you to be. And friend, that's the mark of a warrior on this grand becoming journey. Don't give up. Don't quit. I'm right here fighting with you. You can do this. You can choose to be her.

After my Dad said those 16 game-changing words, I immediately put his reminder in front of my face—on sticky notes, in my journal, and eventually it landed in ink on my right arm as my fourth tattoo. That simple statement has become the "how" for my word: becoming. In 2012, "becoming" became my mantra; and in 2016, "choose to be her" became my battle cry.

Becoming isn't easy. There isn't a formula or "three easy steps," although many days I wish there was. Becoming is a daily choice. It's discovered in and lived out by waking up, lacing up your warrior boots, putting one foot in front of the other, trusting God with each next step, choosing to be her and being who God made you to be with each breath.

We don't have the whole story figured out. We can only live in today's page in the journey. But we always, always have the choice to unlock the prison door we keep ourselves behind, letting external pressure fall to the wayside, and focus on choosing to be her.

Warrior friend, who do you want to be?

What's the first thought that comes to mind? Don't overthink this. Today, I pray I'm looking you in the eyes through this page, reminding you of the truth that woke me up before what could have been a dangerous downward spiral. Wherever you are, no matter what you're facing, *warrior friend: you know who you want to be. You just have to choose to be her.*

Will you?

look what you made me do.

"To be yourself in a world that is constantly trying to make you something else, is the greatest accomplishment."
- Ralph Waldo Emerson

I almost had a heart attack watching one of my absolute favorite artists disappear from social media. Twitter went to war debating whether Taylor Swift was retiring or secretly planning the ultimate comeback as her social media feeds overnight went dark. I crossed my fingers and hoped my go-to jam session singer wouldn't be calling it a day on her career... because I mean, I need more T. Swift albums in my life!

Not long after her disappearance, Taylor shared with fans that a single was coming and the excitement started building. I woke up on that anticipated Friday like many other Swift fans and immediately listened to her new single. I bobbed my head trying to get in the groove of the new tune, but the lyrics struck me; and for a while, I just didn't know what to think as I heard Taylor declare, "*look what you made me do.*"

Days later fans including myself, were glued to the next Taylor release as we watched the official music video reveal. As I saw her anger spew across my screen and heard this repeated statement, "*look what you made me do*," it got me thinking about my story.

Do I live in the posture of pointing my finger at others saying *look what you made me do?*, or do I live in the confidence of choosing to be who God made me to be?

As a little girl, my Dad reminded me often, "Emily, you can't control what happens to you, but you can control what happens in you." A lot is happening around us all the time—we all wake up to the same news, and it seems as if we're constantly waking up to one new story after another. And that doesn't even include our personal day-to-day—from sitting in that creative meeting and your idea not being chosen; to not feeling valued by your boss; to not understanding what your role really is; to getting the doctors report you never wanted to hear; to that argument you had with your spouse as you walked out the door to drop the kids off at school. We can't control what happens to us and around us, how people respond or don't respond, but we sure can control what happens in us. And it all starts with knowing Whose we are and who we are.

There's a guy in the Bible who really lived this—he knew what it was to experience the worst happening to you, yet never wavering from being who God made him to be. Throughout Joseph's story, we see a collision of identity between two central types of characters—those who live their lives pointing their fingers declaring: *look what you made me do*, and Joseph, who consistently stays rooted in who He is and Whose he is.

Let's jump in to Joseph's story in Genesis 37 verse 1:

> Jacob lived in the land where his father had stayed, the land of
> Canaan. 2 This is the account of Jacob's family line. Joseph, a
> young man of seventeen, was tending the flocks with his brothers,
> the sons of Bilhah and the sons of Zilpah, his father's wives, and
> he brought their father a bad report about them. 3 Now Israel
> loved Joseph more than any of his other sons, because he had
> been born to him in his old age; and he made an ornate robe for
> him. 4 When his brothers saw that their father loved him more

> than any of them, they hated him and could not speak a kind word to him. [5] Joseph had a dream, and when he told it to his brothers, they hated him all the more. 6 He said to them, "Listen to this dream I had: [7] We were binding sheaves of grain out in the field when suddenly my sheaf rose and stood upright, while your sheaves gathered around mine and bowed down to it." [8] His brothers said to him, "Do you intend to reign over us? Will you actually rule us?" And they hated him all the more because of his dream and what he had said. [9] Then he had another dream, and he told it to his brothers. "Listen," he said, "I had another dream, and this time the sun and moon and eleven stars were bowing down to me." [10] When he told his father as well as his brothers, his father rebuked him and said, "What is this dream you had? Will your mother and I and your brothers actually come and bow down to the ground before you?" [11] His brothers were jealous of him, but his father kept the matter in mind.
> (Genesis 37:1-11, NIV)

In this first chunk of Joseph's story, we learn a lot about who Joseph is—

- He was his Dad's favorite, and his brothers hated him for it.
- He was a dreamer, and his brothers hated him even more.
- Even though he knew his brothers hated him, it never stopped him from dreaming and being who God made him to be.

In these first 11 verses, we immediately see a clash of identities—1: Joseph's brothers, who are so blinded by their jealousy and hatred that they don't know who they are; and 2: Joseph, who doesn't allow his brothers' jealousy to deter him from being who God made him to be.

It's interesting to note that Joseph didn't dream once, experience rejection from his brothers, and then give up... no! He dreamed, he experienced rejection, and he kept on dreaming. When we know Whose we are and who we are, we can keep on dreaming no matter what those around us do or don't do, say or don't say.

Here's the tension: will I believe in myself and my dream and keep dreaming even when no one else believes in me? When they criticize me? When they laugh at me? Don't let anyone stop you from dreaming big and sharing the God-dreams God is inviting you to be a part of. When you know Whose you are and who you are, and you're choosing to be who God made you to be, you dream freely and without reservation.

This is how BecomingMe.TV began. As a junior in high school, I entered Focus On The Family's annual Brio Girl contest, a nation-wide search for a high school girl to regularly contribute to *Brio Magazine* through her very own monthly column. Simultaneously, I started a personal blog, sharing my thoughts and learnings. As the contest progressed, I made it to the top four finalists... but that's as far as I got. I didn't win. Initially, my eleventh grade heart concluded I wasn't as good of a writer as I thought, questioning whether writing was a part of God's plan for me or not. Rather than staying there, I shook the doubts off and kept going. I kept writing, and now over a decade later, that little, personal blog has become a global community empowering people to become who God made them to be, sharing hundreds of video interviews, partnering with CRTVCHURCH, launching a podcast, hosting conferences, and the writing of this book! None of this would have happened if I would have given up when I didn't win the title Brio Girl.

What could God do in and through your story if you dare to keep dreaming?

Let's keep going in Joseph's story by diving into verse 17:

> So Joseph went after his brothers and found them near Dothan. [18] But they saw him in the distance, and before he reached them, they plotted to kill him. [19] "Here comes that dreamer!"

> they said to each other. [20] "Come now, let's kill him and throw
> him into one of these cisterns and say that a ferocious animal
> devoured him. Then we'll see what comes of his dreams." [21] When
> Reuben heard this, he tried to rescue him from their hands. "Let's
> not take his life," he said. [22] "Don't shed any blood. Throw him into
> this cistern here in the wilderness, but don't lay a hand on him."
> Reuben said this to rescue him from them and take him back to
> his father. [23] So when Joseph came to his brothers, they stripped
> him of his robe—the ornate robe he was wearing— [24] and they
> took him and threw him into the cistern. The cistern was empty;
> there was no water in it. [25] As they sat down to eat their meal,
> they looked up and saw a caravan of Ishmaelites coming from
> Gilead. Their camels were loaded with spices, balm and myrrh, and
> they were on their way to take them down to Egypt. [26] Judah said
> to his brothers, "What will we gain if we kill our brother and cover
> up his blood? [27] Come, let's sell him to the Ishmaelites and not lay
> our hands on him; after all, he is our brother, our own flesh and
> blood." His brothers agreed. [28] So when the Midianite merchants
> came by, his brothers pulled Joseph up out of the cistern and
> sold him for twenty shekels of silver to the Ishmaelites, who took
> him to Egypt. [29] When Reuben returned to the cistern and saw
> that Joseph was not there, he tore his clothes. [30] He went back
> to his brothers and said, "The boy isn't there! Where can I turn
> now?" [31] Then they got Joseph's robe, slaughtered a goat and
> dipped the robe in the blood. [32] They took the ornate robe back
> to their father and said, "We found this. Examine it to see whether
> it is your son's robe."
> (Genesis 37:17-32, NIV)

Joseph, *look what you made us do*! His brothers were so blinded by their hatred and jealousy that they literally sat over lunch debating: do we kill our brother or do we sell him into slavery?

In my experience, whenever I've been jealous of someone or think they have it better off than me, I'm not in tune with who I am, I'm missing out on who God made me to be. Joseph's brothers didn't know who they were, and they spent all their time blinded by hatred for who they considered the "golden child," rather than owning who they were made to be and celebrating who God made their brother to be.

When you and I live rooted in jealousy and hatred towards someone else, we act out, pointing at those around us with our words, attitudes, and actions, figuratively or literally saying "*look what you made me do,*" rather than living confidently in who God made us to be. Can you imagine how different this story would be if Joseph's brothers hadn't been jealous of him in the first place? If they all would have chosen to be who God made them to be, rather than worrying about what they deemed as unjust or not fair?

How different would our stories be if rather than scrolling through Instagram and being jealous of *their* gifts and talents and stories, we lived confidently in who we were made to be and took our own next steps?

So Joseph is sold into slavery and has every right to be mad, angry, and throw a temper tantrum, but we don't see that happen. Rather than seeing a guy driven by emotions, we see a man rooted in Whose he is and who he is...

Let's dive back in in Genesis 39 verse 1:

> Now Joseph had been taken down to Egypt. Potiphar, an
> Egyptian who was one of Pharaoh's officials, the captain of the
> guard, bought him from the Ishmaelites who had taken him
> there. [2] The Lord was with Joseph so that he prospered, and he
> lived in the house of his Egyptian master. [3] When his master saw
> that the Lord was with him and that the Lord gave him success
> in everything he did, [4] Joseph found favor in his eyes and became
> his attendant. Potiphar put him in charge of his household, and
> he entrusted to his care everything he owned. [5] From the time
> he put him in charge of his household and of all that he owned,
> the Lord blessed the household of the Egyptian because of
> Joseph. The blessing of the Lord was on everything Potiphar had,
> both in the house and in the field. [6] So Potiphar left everything he
> had in Joseph's care; with Joseph in charge, he did not concern
> himself with anything except the food he ate.
> (Genesis 39:1-6, NIV)

Did you see an angry, bitter guy in these six verses? Nope? Me neither! I see a guy who understands that while he can't control what happens to him, he can control what happens in him. He knows who he is and Whose he is and doesn't waver.

Let's continue the story in the end of verses 6-7:

> Now Joseph was well-built and handsome, [7] and after a while his master's wife took notice of Joseph and said, "Come to bed with me!" [8] But he refused. "With me in charge," he told her, "my master does not concern himself with anything in the house; everything he owns he has entrusted to my care. [9] No one is greater in this house than I am. My master has withheld nothing from me except you, because you are his wife. How then could I do such a wicked thing and sin against God?" [10] And though she spoke to Joseph day after day, he refused to go to bed with her or even be with her. [11] One day he went into the house to attend to his duties, and none of the household servants was inside. [12] She caught him by his cloak and said, "Come to bed with me!" But he left his cloak in her hand and ran out of the house. [13] When she saw that he had left his cloak in her hand and had run out of the house, [14] she called her household servants. "Look," she said to them, "this Hebrew has been brought to us to make sport of us! He came in here to sleep with me, but I screamed. [15] When he heard me scream for help, he left his cloak beside me and ran out of the house." [16] She kept his cloak beside her until his master came home. [17] Then she told him this story: "That Hebrew slave you brought us came to me to make sport of me.[18] But as soon as I screamed for help, he left his cloak beside me and ran out of the house." [19] When his master heard the story his wife told him, saying, "This is how your slave treated me," he burned with anger. [20] Joseph's master took him and put him in prison, the place where the king's prisoners were confined.
> (Genesis 39:6-20, NIV)

Does this dude ever get a break?! Joseph has been sold into slavery by his brothers, he stays true to who he is and prospers working in Potipher's house, and now Potipher's wife accuses him of assaulting her? Once again in Joseph's story, we see the stark comparison between someone who has no clue who they are and is content to live in the posture of the blame game, pointing to everyone else around them saying, "look what you made me do," and we see Joseph standing strong.

Joseph's story doesn't end with this second attempt to derail his life. Take a look at what we find in verse 20:

> But while Joseph was there in the prison, [21] the Lord was with him; he showed him kindness and granted him favor in the eyes of the prison warden. [22] So the warden put Joseph in charge of all those held in the prison, and he was made responsible for all that was done there. [23] The warden paid no attention to anything under Joseph's care, because the Lord was with Joseph and gave him success in whatever he did.
> (Genesis 39:20-23, NIV)

Did you catch that? The Lord was with him. God granted Him favor in prison, where for the second time he has been betrayed, set up, and accused.

It's easy to spot someone who's been in the presence of Jesus. They have a peace embedded in their foundation, they're confident and secure, they walk with Jesus. I think Joseph walked a lot like that.

This is the starting point to getting to know who we are. If we don't know our Creator, how could we ever really know ourselves? To know who you are, you must first know Whose you are. Joseph understood that. And Jesus being in him, with him and for him, is what ultimately gave him the strength to live confidently in who he was created to be.

Joseph's story continues in prison and we read in Genesis 41 that he eventually is called into Pharaoh's presence to interpret Pharoah's dreams and, in turn, ended up developing a game plan to see Egypt through years of famine. Y'all, a guy sold as a slave by his own brothers, accused of assault, and forgotten in prison becomes second in command in the land of Egypt... the right hand man to Pharaoh. How does that happen?

Joseph knew Whose he was and who he was.

And he never, ever stopped being himself.

Is this how we live when life is crazy or when life is awesome? Do we stay rooted in Whose we are and who we are?

Joseph didn't have a fancy three-step outline to success at being himself. He just chose to be him. He stayed in tune with his Creator and never, ever stopped becoming who God made Him to be.

I love how Galatians 6 in The Message translation encourages us to choose to be ourselves:

> Make a careful exploration of who you are and the work you have been given, and then sink yourself into that. Don't be impressed with yourself. Don't compare yourself with others. Each of you must take responsibility for doing the creative best you can with your own life.
>
> (Galatians 6:4-5, MSG)

How can you know who you are and become more in tune with yourself? Live Galatians 6:4-5. Make a careful exploration of who you are and the work you have been given, and then sink yourself into that. And at the end of our stories, may we declare with all our might... not "*look what you made me do,*" but "*here I am being only who God made me to be and look what my God has done.*"

Joseph's story ends in Genesis 45:5-8, as he's reunited with his brothers, and the conversation goes like this:

> Do not be distressed and do not be angry with yourselves for selling me here, because it was to save lives that God sent me ahead of you. [6] For two years now there has been famine in the land, and for the next five years there will be no plowing and reaping. [7] But God sent me ahead of you to preserve for you a remnant on earth and to save your lives by a great deliverance. [8] "So then, it was not you who sent me here, but God.

BUT GOD SENT ME.

This is how I want the end of my becoming story to look. No matter what people do or don't do, say or don't say, I can look back with confidence knowing I didn't waver from being who God made me to be and that God worked through me, and it all started because I just chose to be her.

Warrior friend, you know who you want to be. Will you choose to be you?

what's your why?

"If we want to feel an undying passion for our work, if we want to feel we are contributing to something bigger than ourselves, we all need to know our WHY."

- Simon Sinek

W*hat gets you out of bed in the morning?*

It's a simple question, yet often we have such a hard time answering it, pinpointing that passion and dream defined as our "why."

14 years ago, I pushed "publish" on my first blog post in this house. In 2007, as a junior in high school, I didn't have a strategic decade-long plan mapping out where I would take my little blog—I just knew I loved writing. Writing has always been my outlet, my passion, how I process and understand my becoming journey.

Little did I know that my blog would transform into a beautiful resource and community for thousands of women around the world. I was just tapping into what I love and what helps me personally on my becoming journey.

In 2014, I called my warrior friend Amy and asked, "Hey! What would you think about coming over to my apartment and us filming your story, how you're becoming who God made you to be, and then sharing that on my blog?" She said yes, we filmed her story, and Becoming Stories were born. Did I know in 2014 that just seven years later, we would have filmed and shared over 100 Becoming Stories? Nope. I just knew I saw women becoming who God made them to be all around me—women who are strong, who are beautiful, and whose stories are so very important—and I wanted to share those stories.

I think we discover our "why" in the seemingly insignificant moments where we say "yes," trusting God with the next step in front of us. Pushing publish on a blog? Interviewing a friend? Pretty simple moments. However, they've changed my life, and they're changing the lives of countless people on their own becoming journeys too.

In the moment, becoming who God made you to be just seems like hard work, life, steps. However, looking back, I can see how each step I've taken on my becoming journey has led me to where I am today, discovering more and more of my why, my purpose, my driving force. It would be easy to define my purpose as being a writer or communicator or storyteller; but, my purpose, my why, goes so much deeper than something I do. My why drills down to the core of who I am: a woman becoming who God made her to be with all she's got, and who wakes up every day to help people become who God made them to be, too. That's it, that's my answer, that's why I get out of bed every day.

I didn't discover my why in one big moment, but rather in many little moments over time. But I know with everything in me this is who I was created to be, what I was created to do.

Warrior friend, what gets you out of bed in the morning? Looking back on your journey so far, what handful of seemingly insignificant moments have made the most profound impact on your story? Dissect those moments—what made them stand out to you? I believe you'll begin to discover your why there. And when you do, your heart will skip a beat as you see with fresh eyes who God has created you to be and this grand purpose He has birthed in and through your life.

Run after your why. Run after becoming who God made you to be with every fiber in your being... I'm here running with you.

I am designed
on purpose and
for purpose by God.

female.

"I would like to be known as an intelligent woman, a courageous woman, a loving woman, a woman who teaches by being."
- Maya Angelou

I *love* warrior chick movies. There's just something about watching a woman overcome some crazy-hard obstacle, and come out victorious.

When Keith Urban debuted his song "Female" at the CMA Awards in November 2017, I sat upright in my chair. I stopped scrolling through Instagram and listened as I saw words describing what it means to be "female" flicker across the stage.

The words I read cut straight to my heart and sat there for days, weeks, and months after that awards show.

Growing up, my Daddy taught my sister, Katie, and I that we could do, accomplish, and be anything we dreamed of doing and being. I grew up believing that and dreaming big dreams ranging from being a veterinarian to a speech writer to even the President of the United States. It wasn't until my early twenties that I became aware of the cultural confusion surrounding just what it means to be "female". Leaving a strategic planning meeting one day, a co-worker made the observation that I was the only female in the room, and that since my leadership, more women were beginning to step up to and lead. Because of how my Daddy had consistently poured confidence into me and my sister, this surprised me, and for a while I didn't understand why women held back. I didn't understand why people were confused as to what a woman could accomplish or who she could become.

Then I heard Keith Urban's song, and the lyrics reminded me of what God has breathed into our bones from the start: *baby girl, it's not what you do that makes you female. It's who you are.*

When we live from the core of who God made us to be, daily choosing to be her, we come out victorious, no matter what obstacle stands in our way.

Who did God uniquely design females to be? Two distinguishers stand out from the first woman, Eve. First, she was created to be a *partner* to Adam. Second, she was designed to be a *producer* of new life.

> The Lord God said, "It is not good for the man to be alone. I will make a helper suitable for him." [19] Now the Lord God had formed out of the ground all the wild animals and all the birds in the sky. He brought them to the man to see what he would name them; and whatever the man called each living creature, that was its name. [20] So the man gave names to all the livestock, the birds in the sky and all the wild animals. But for Adam no suitable helper was found. [21] So the Lord God caused the man to fall into a deep sleep; and while he was sleeping, he took one of the man's ribs and then closed up the place with flesh. [22] Then the Lord God made a woman from the rib he had taken out of the man, and he brought her to the man. (Genesis 2:18-22, NIV)

Notice God didn't craft Eve from Adam's pinky toe, his elbow, or any other part of his body for that matter. Intentionally, Eve was formed from Adam's rib cage—his side—placing Eve's position directly next to him, not above or beneath Adam. She was designed to be his helper, his partner, to make him and the world around them better.

It's also important to identify that Eve wasn't designed to be Adam's competitor either. Eve was designed—and we as women are designed—to complement and partner with those around us... not compete, belittle or shut down. Walking confidently as the female God designed you, me... us... to be is rooted in our identity in Christ. Being "female" has nothing to do with the very things causing confusion and tension swirling around us—salaries, job titles, being invited to the table, having someone speak life and confidence into you or not. Yes, can and should we pursue big dreams and break glass ceilings? Absolutely! But only in a way that lifts all people up. There's no strength in being female if it means we have to tear down those we were designed to partner with in the first place.

Warrior friend, if you hear anything in the few pages of this chapter, hear this: you are not the salary you make, the job title you have, whether you grew up believing you could be anything you wanted to be or not. You are designed on purpose and for purpose by God. He designed you as a partner and producer. Don't ever doubt your value.

Genesis 3:16 unpacks the moments after Adam and Eve disobeyed God in the garden, outlining the consequences each would face. For Eve? Childbirth would be painful. Ouch... while the pain of this curse weighs heavy, there is a blessing hidden within. *Females give birth to new life.*

Hear me: birthing new life doesn't always look like bringing a human into this world. Producing new life is discovered in choosing to extend kind words, and shutting down gossip; walking in peace, not drama and chaos; taking your next step today, not procrastinating what you know you should do; investing in your local church, not sitting on the sidelines; encouraging those around you, not competing with them; and sometimes birthing new life looks like bringing a newborn into the world or adopting a child to raise, helping them become who they were made to be, too.

Warrior women, we are *partners* and we are *producers*. And at the root of it all, we have the power to choose to be both, or not. We choose to partner with those around us, or leave them alone, fending for themselves. We choose to produce life with the words we speak, the people we mentor, the opportunities we step into, or not.

> Today I have given you the **choice** between life and death, between blessings and curses. Now I call on heaven and earth to witness the **choice** you make. Oh, that you would **choose life**, so that you and your descendants might live!
>
> (Deuteronomy 30:19, NLT, emphasis added)

What does it mean to be female? Choosing to be who God made you to be. The choice is always up to you, and only you. Friend, you are a warrior woman. You are a partner. You are a producer. You are female.

expecting Jesus to show up.

"If God doesn't show up, it's game over, lights out."
- Mark Cummins

Growing up a pastor's kid, I've often heard my Daddy lead church staff and our church family with this phrase: "If God doesn't show up, it's game over, lights out." Seeing this consistent model of complete, open-handed, dependent trust in God to show up, has always encouraged me to be expectant for Jesus. However, I'm learning what that means on a personal level.

In Luke 2, a group of shepherds were going about their everyday lives when something crazy out-of-the-ordinary happened. I can just imagine them tending the sheep, maybe making small talk, and then boom—an angel drops in on their conversation and tells them about this newborn baby who was going to save the world. They listened, were a tiny bit terrified (or maybe a lot), experienced an epic worship moment with a whole host of angels, and then were left blinking, looking at each other wondering "what just happened?!"

I imagine this happening in my ordinary life. I'm going about my day, knocking out my Asana to-do list, when boom an angel drops by my desk and tells me something crazy-out-of-the-ordinary is happening. I'd probably be a whole-lot terrified and wondering "what is happening?!"

I love what the shepherds did next:

> When the angels had returned to heaven, the shepherds said to each other, "Let's go to Bethlehem! Let's see this thing that has happened, which the Lord has told us about."
> (Luke 2:15, NLT)

They heard God was up to something and immediately went into action—they went to see with their own eyes what God was doing.

When I hear God's up to something and I see Him at work, I want to live with the posture the shepherds had that starry night—I want to move. I want to spring into action, take that next step, and go see with my own eyes what God is doing. I don't want to just hear about it secondhand. I want to be up in on the story of hope that God is writing all over the world.

But the shepherds' story doesn't end with them going to check out what God was up to...

> They hurried to the village and found Mary and Joseph. And there was the baby, lying in the manger. [17] After seeing him, the shepherds told everyone what had happened and what the angel had said to them about this child. [18] All who heard the shepherds' story were astonished, [19] but Mary kept all these things in her heart and thought about them often. [20] The shepherds went back to their flocks, glorifying and praising God for all they had heard and seen. It was just as the angel had told them.
> (Luke 2:16-20, NLT)

The shepherds went to see what God was doing, saw the baby Jesus with their own eyes, and then went and told everyone what they had seen. And after sharing their experience? They went back about their everyday, ordinary lives, but this time with a totally different mindset. Now, in their everyday, ordinary work they were "glorifying and praising God for all they had heard and seen." (Luke 2:20, NLT)

That's how I want to live. I want to live hearing from God, but not just hearing...expecting Him to show up. I want to be in the middle of my everyday, ordinary work and see how God is moving all around me with my own two eyes. I want to see it, and then share it with those around me. And I don't want to ever walk away the same. I want God showing up to change me from the inside out, causing me to walk back to the desk of life glorifying and praising God, and then expecting Him to show up again and again and again.

You see, I think—and this is just what I think—that the angel showed up to those shepherds that night because they were expecting something to happen in their world. They were ready for God to move, to show up, to save His people. And because they had expectant hearts, they were able to hear that God was up to something, go see it for themselves, share the hope of Jesus with everyone around them, and then never live the same again.

That is what living expectant for Jesus is all about. *That* is what my Daddy has always meant when he says, "If God doesn't show up, it's game over, lights out." He's living expectant for God to show up, ready to hear what He's up to, see it, share it and never live the same.

That's how I want to live—expectant for God to move, to show up here in my every day, ordinary life, for me to get in on it and see it for myself, share the hope I've experienced in Jesus with those around me, and never, ever be the same.

experience is what you make it.

"Believe you can and you're halfway there."

- Theodore Roosevelt

How I see things matters. And I'm not referring to having 20/20 eye sight here. The way I choose to engage with the circumstances and people around me flows from my vision, my mindset, my perspective, my heart.

I remember driving home after one of my first days at a new school. I hated it. I didn't want to go back. I was discouraged, questioning if I had made the right academic decision. Had I picked the wrong school? Was my entire future at stake? Would I make any friends? Enjoy any of my classes?

After chatting with my Daddy, he offered a statement of advice that I've treasured ever since: "Experience is what you make it."

You know what goes hand-in-hand with experience? My thoughts. I choose what I think, what I dwell on, what I meditate on, what I obsess over. Anytime I embark on a negative downward spiral, I can always pinpoint the moment of attitude change to a negative thought I allowed to take the control center of my mind hostage.

Why didn't I like my first day at that new school? I had already decided in my mind I wasn't going to like it. I had only experienced half of my courses on that first day and hadn't given any new friendships a chance. I stared at the swirling world of "new" circling around me and immediately decided I didn't want to try, I didn't want to make it a fun, memorable experience. I had given up before I even tried.

Experience is what you make it.

Day two at that school was a different story. I looked at my environment in a different light. Rather than seeing a bleak, rocky semester ahead of me, I saw a plethora of opportunity at my fingertips. I saw thousands of people walking past me, thousands of opportunities for new friendships and new memories. I saw the opportunity to receive a top-notch education, the opportunity to truly study, learn, and grow, preparing for God's next best step for my life.

It's been years since that first day of classes at a school I initially decided I didn't like. And you know what? Some of my favorite memories from my entire educational journey are at that school. Some of the primary friends I keep in touch with from that season of my life are from that school. The first editor of this very book is a friend I made at that school. Some of the most foundational things I learned about myself and who God is shaping me to be were at that school. And I could have missed it entirely if I hadn't changed my mindset.

I control my thoughts. We control what we see, what we think, what we experience. Warrior friend, we control what takes up residence in our heart and mind.

Check out these verses:

> Take captive every thought to make it obedient to Christ. (2 Corinthians 10:5, NIV)

> Whatever is true, whatever is noble, whatever is right, whatever is pure, whatever is lovely, whatever is admirable—if anything is excellent or praiseworthy—think about such things.
> (Philippians 4:8, NIV)

No matter what you face today, take a step back and choose how you want to see it, how you want to experience it. Do you want to experience the glass-is-half-empty side of life or the glass-is-half-full side? Ultimately, the choice is up to you, because experience is what you make it.

when the lemons come, I'll be ready.

making lemonade.

"When everything seems to be going against you, remember that the airplane takes off against the wind, not with it."

- Henry Ford

Choosing to be you isn't easy. It's easy to write about, sing songs about, and declare proclamations of your choice with bracelets and t-shirts. But living it, well, that's a whole different ball game.

Here's a question I've been wrestling with: *how much would it take to break me?* In the midst of the tough stuff of life, I find myself wondering what my limit is, what my breaking point would be. When life throws hundreds of lemons my way, making lemonade isn't always the first thing that crosses my mind. Lately, the first question popping to the forefront of my thoughts is centered around how many more lemons I can take.

Proverbs 24:10 stops me in my tracks and exposes that I've been asking the wrong question entirely:

> "If you fall to pieces in a crisis, there wasn't much to you in the first place."
> (Proverbs 24:10, MSG)

My question in the midst of the battle has been centered around the aftermath—the getting out of the battle alive part—when, in truth, I should be focusing on a much more vital question: ***what did I do to prepare for the battle?***

Foundation is everything. How someone trains or didn't train makes a world of difference in combat. And here's the thing about training—I can't hide if I prepared or didn't prepare. On game day, it will show up. Ask any athlete and they'll be the first to tell you: a lack of training off the field shows up on the field. The same is true in life.

While I've been dodging lemons left and right, I missed out on the opportunity of making gallons of lemonade. I could have been sitting poolside with a refreshing glass of lemonade and the latest Nicholas Sparks book in hand. But today, I'm re-assessing my foundation. I'm lacing up my boots and headed into training because the next time lemons are thrown my way, I want to be ready to make lemonade and not dodge perfectly good ingredients for growth.

Proverbs 24 challenges us:

> "It's better to be wise than strong; intelligence outranks muscle any day. Strategic planning is the key to warfare; to win, you need a lot of good counsel."
> (Proverbs 24:5-6, MSG)

Training isn't about physical fitness. It's about my mental aptitude and being ready for the moments that threaten to knock me to the ground—the moments when the guy you thought you would marry breaks your heart; when your hard-earned savings are wiped away by scammers; when your parents' marriage of 50 years crumbles into a divorce; when your best friend shares the news she is suffering from cancer; when you total your car; when you undergo emergency surgery. Being ready for the difficult moments of life stems from how I strategically planned in advance to walk through them. And how do I do that? By surrounding myself with truth. The truth of God's Word and solid advice.

One of my favorite verses is found in James and lays out pretty clear instructions for suiting up for battle:

> "Get down on your knees before the Master; it's the only way you'll get on your feet."
> (James 4:10, MSG)

The only way I'll get on my feet is by starting on my knees. I can't show up to battle alone anymore. That's a guaranteed way for me to not only burn out, but to also lose the fight entirely. If I'm not filling myself with the truth of Jesus and what He is saying to me first, there's no way I can show up ready to fight and make some great lemonade.

Today, I'm kneeling. I'm suiting up in my armor. I'm diving into the Word of God and planning for war. This time, when the lemons come, I'll be ready. No more counting and wishing they would disappear, slow down, or stop. Rather, my battle cry is "Keep the lemons comin' because this girl wants to make some scrumptious lemonade."

becoming allie.

This chapter was written by a fellow warrior with you in mind.

In much of my journey of becoming, I've let my grief hang like a cloud over my head. And it's easy to do that when four of the people you love most in the world, and yourself, all have incurable diseases. While most of our diseases are thankfully not terminal, my Dad's cancer took him from us in 2014.

When my Dad died, I let my grief wash over my life and turn into anger. Not just grumbling and irritability—white hot rage... at God. I couldn't understand why, after all the things my family had been through and everything good my Dad had done, God would not heal him here on this earth.

That anger against God quickly turned into anger against the Church. In confusion, I wrestled watching people in the church I love declaring what they were against culturally rather than what we are for—as a Christ follower, I am for showing compassion and love to all people to discover the hope we have in Christ. My feelings compounded as I struggled feeling unsupported in my grief over my dad.

I knew something had to change. Little by little, I started diving into the Bible—especially Jesus's words and life. That was the Jesus

I loved. Not the one being represented by the people around me. *Not the one being represented by me.*

And there were two things I learned.

One, seeing God's goodness throughout the Bible helped me understand God's goodness in my own life and world. I knew God was telling me that if He loves the Church—and He does—then I needed to love it too and do that by being a part of it. God reassured me of His goodness, even in the midst of my anger.

Even in the midst of my grief.

Second, I learned that grief is not a process to go through and get over. Grief is necessary to help us find the beauty and joy in life.

I've found that no one really helps you know quite what to expect with grief. Grief over someone you love dying—now, that's expected. Grief over a friendship falling out, a lifelong diagnosis, a lost dream—that's the grief you don't expect.

I also never knew that grief never really fully goes away. That anger I thought I was over... I feel it well up inside every time I hear of another person with a cancer diagnosis. Every time I have a bad diabetes day. Every job rejection or missed promotion. Five steps forward, one step back.

I used to have the misconception that you were supposed to get over your grief. That you weren't supposed to feel the deep pit of sadness in the bottom of your chest every time you look at old photographs or laugh about a funny memory. That you weren't supposed to burst into tears on an anniversary or just a random day with a little nostalgia.

But what I've learned is that grief never goes away. And I think that's okay. I always felt like I was not making progress, but now I see that progress is learning how to navigate living a joyful, meaningful life, in the middle of grief. I understand that acceptance isn't getting over the grief—it's giving myself those moments to mourn, but not letting my anger get the best of me and turn me bitter.

Jesus's own life helped me understand grief. Jesus grieved over a friend that He knew was going to come back from the dead. With His almighty power and knowledge, He still wept. Before His own death, knowing the life and freedom it would bring to the world, He grieved for the sacrifice He knew was necessary but also for those that hurt and rejected Him. Jesus lived His life with grief—fully human and fully God—but through those moments some of the most beautiful things happened.

I'll let you in on something: I still don't understand why my Dad wasn't healed. But I now know I don't need to understand to know God's goodness. My Dad believed it, up until his very last day. And I believe it now too—to the very core of who I am.

After working through my anger and understanding my grief, I started to heal my relationship with God—and through that started to heal my relationship with Church and other Christians. My grief was still there, but it wasn't hanging over my head in a cloud of sorrow and anger. Through some of the most painful parts of my life, God continued to show up for me, love me, and guide me into continuing to become the person He has called me to be.

And that's what becoming is all about. It's not about being perfect or getting it right all the time. It's not about always being happy or rushing to get over every sad or negative emotion. It's about allowing God to use some of the worst, most painful parts of life to mold us into something beautiful. Moving through grief into joy. Jars of clay, holding treasure.

warrior steps.

(1) Who do you want to be?

(2) Do you want to live your life pointing your finger, declaring "*look what you made me do*!" OR do you want to walk confidently choosing to be who God made you to be? If you're committed to the later, pick a symbol to remind you to choose to be you. For me, it's a key tattoo on the inside of my arm. Perhaps for you it will be a piece of jewelry, a sticky note on a mirror, a key chain, or something else!

Pick your reminder, snap a photo or video, and share on social media tagging @emilybcummins & @becomingme.tv — I can't wait to cheer you on!

(3) What's your why?

(4) Write Deuteronomy 30:19 in the NLT version on a sticky note and put it somewhere to remind you that God designed you to be a partner and producer!

(5) Do you expect Jesus to show up in your every day moments? If you don't, pray and ask God to shift and adjust your heart to one of expectation and awareness of His presence every, single day.

(6) How do you want to experience life? With a glass-half-empty or glass-half-full vantage point? Only you can decide... experience is what you make it.

(7) The next time a challenging moment occurs in your becoming story, remind yourself to live James 4:10—getting on your knees before God asking Him to strengthen you to stand. Place this reminder from God's Word in a place you will see it and be reminded to suit up for battle.

warrior.

"She never seemed shattered; to me, she was a breathtaking mosaic of the battles she's won."
- Anonymous

now i'm a warrior.

"Be a warrior, not a worrier."

- Anonymous

For the last few years I have been obsessed—and I mean literally *obsessed*—with any and every female warrior story I could get my hands on. I've committed to devouring stacks of books, scoured the Internet, and repeatedly found my eyes glued to Netflix's array of warrior flicks. Let's just say gals like Katniss Everdeen, Calamity Jane, Mulan, Beatrice Prior, and Queen Elsa have become some of my closest besties. I've consumed incredible books like *Girls with Swords* and *Lioness Arising* by Lisa Bevere, *Let's All Be Brave* by Annie Downs, *Warrior Chicks* by Holly Wagner, *The Fight to Flourish* by Jennie Lusko, and *Fighting Forward* by Hannah Brencher. I've had countless dance parties to songs like "Titatium," "Fight Song," "Roar," and "Stronger." I even have a warrior tattoo on my bicep.

And in the midst of my dance sessions, poolside reading, and Netflix binging, a common thread emerged in these leading ladies' plot lines: they were feisty, fierce, bold, and confident. They overcame their fears; they rallied people who had given up, and re-introduced them to hope; they kicked butt and took names;

they stared death in the face... and they won. They were lionhearted.

> **Lionhearted** *(adjective)*:
> To be constantly challenging oneself; taking every single opportunity without regrets; learning, developing and seeing beauty in all kinds of moments in life no matter how big or small they may be; knowing what you're worth, treating yourself like you deserve to be treated; simply, just being you and being brave; like a lion, you fight for what you stand for; a lionheart would never give up on her dreams; exceptionally courageous or brave.
> (Adapted from Urban Dictionary)

It wasn't really a coincidence or sign of boredom that led me to these heroines' front doors. Deep down I have been aching for something more, for a bravery and strength to rise up within me, within my own story. I have been ravenously devouring the stories of warriors, hoping I would be inspired to be a warrior too.

Alongside their brave acts of heroism and shiny swords, the women I have so passionately been studying have an additional common thread that reaches beyond their sleek confidence and into the depths of pain, heartache, betrayal, and shame. My feisty heroines probably wouldn't classify themselves as brave or strong or fierce. In fact, they might argue the exact opposite. They would defend that they were simply stepping up in response to the cards life dealt them, to what needed to be done in order to survive, and to protect those they love.

There isn't glory without guts. There isn't a warrior without something to fight for. Gumption and pain go hand-in-hand. Without the affliction, misery, falseness and deception, we would have no need for spunk and courage.

Deep down, I don't think God made us to simply coast. I believe He fashioned us with incredible purpose and armed us with a tenacious strength we often don't even realize we have within us.

Before His crucifixion, Jesus empowered and equipped His disciples—and He's equipping us still today:

> "I've told you all this so that trusting me, you will be unshakeable and assured, deeply at peace. In this godless world you will continue to experience difficulties. But take heart! I've conquered the world."
> (John 16:33, MSG)

Jesus never mentions a lack of fear in His message to us. Rather, He reaches down and whispers, "Precious warrior daughter, life is going to happen. It's going to hurt. But in the midst of it all, you can live unshakable and assured. You can stand grounded in peace. I've already won."

Maybe living fearless is about embracing the reality that there will be fear and pain and stuff we don't want to walk through, but how, in the midst of it all, we can boldly steep our lives in the grand truth that our God has already won.

So when that friend you thought would stand with you through it all betrays your trust, your world doesn't have to be shaken because we trust in a God bigger than the sting of betrayal; when you receive the phone call from the doctor asking you to come in for just a few more tests because they think they've spotted something, you can rest assured, deeply at peace, because we serve a God who is stronger than the results on a doctor's lab report; when your husband of twenty-something years declares he wants a divorce, you can stand grounded in the truth that you are a loved daughter of the King of kings; when your boss says that you're no longer a good fit for the company or that cuts are being made, you can walk confidently knowing God has fashioned you with purpose; and when the bills are piling up and it seems like this month you just won't be able to make ends meet, you can boldly worship the God who provides.

A warrior is one who drives her stake in the ground, claiming victory over the decisions of yesterday while boldly fixing her eyes on the path ahead. She laces up her boots, brushes the dirt off her face and declares herself to be the beloved warrior God already designed her to be. Warriors embrace a lionhearted stance, declaring war on purposelessness while fighting from the victory that is already ours in Jesus Christ.

May we be women anchored in our beliefs who passionately pursue becoming the women God has made us to be, and may we not be afraid to lace up our boots, because friends, we are warriors.

lacing up your warrior boots in peace.

"To become who God made you to be, you must lace up your warrior boots in peace."

- Emily B. Cummins

In September 2017, I found myself stepping out of one of the most intense weeks of my life. Those of us in Central Florida the week of September 10 experienced true chaos up close and personal as Hurricane Irma made landfall, traveling across our state. Anxiety was high as gas, food, and water shortages rose. My story, however, doesn't start with Irma's landfall. It begins 72 hours earlier.

On September 7, I opened my Bible to Ephesians 6:13-17, and a single verse struck me in a way it never had before.

> [13] Therefore put on the full armor of God, so that when the day of evil comes, you may be able to stand your ground, and after you have done everything, to stand.[14] Stand firm then, with the belt of truth buckled around your waist, with the breastplate of righteousness in place, [15] and with your feet fitted with the readiness that comes from the gospel of peace. [16] In addition to all this, take up the shield of faith, with which you can extinguish

> all the flaming arrows of the evil one. [17] Take the helmet of salvation and the sword of the Spirit, which is the word of God.
> (Ephesians 6:13-17, NIV)

As I read verse 15, I knew I would never be the same: *"...and with your feet fitted with the readiness that comes from the gospel of peace."*

It became clear to me in that moment that one of my personal mantras, "lace up your warrior boots," is more than a symbol of courage or bravery, it's a symbol of peace.

What you dress your feet with is your foundation, the bedrock for how you can stand and fight the battle of becoming who God made you to be. Here in Ephesians 6, God's Word was spelling it out for me so plainly: my foundation, the armor for my feet, for each step I take is peace.

To become who God made me to be, I need to lace up my warrior boots with peace. How ironic. When we step into combat, we're stepping into anything but peace, we're stepping into war.

In 1 Samuel 25, we find Abigail journeying towards David, extending peace to him after her husband stirred up unnecessary chaos. Abigail had no idea how David would respond—would he accept her gift of peace, or reject her offering, hanging on to anger towards her husband's foolishness? While she didn't know what David's response would be, Abigail did not allow uncertainty to delay her. In fact, three times in 1 Samuel 25, we read that Abigail acted "quickly"—she quickly gathered supplies, she quickly traveled towards David, and she quickly extended peace. Abigail was able to act quickly because she was properly suited for battle; she had done the hard work of lacing up her warrior boots in peace before the chaos ever came her way. How do I know this? Just a few verses earlier, we see Abigail's reputation and character precede her.

> She was an intelligent and beautiful woman, but her husband was surly and mean in his dealings...
> (1 Samuel 25:3, NIV)

lacing up your warrior boots in peace.

Warrior friend, to become who God made you to be, like Abigail, you need to lace up your warrior boots with peace.

Little did I know that three days after reading those words in Ephesians 6, after my own discovery of peace, how much I would need to rely on that truth and literally lace up my warrior boots in peace. On Monday, September 11, 2017, my hometown woke up to the aftermath of the hurricane. People slowly began making their way out of their homes, assessing the damage, and seeing how their neighbors had fared.

As the Executive Director at Church of Hope, I went with the Lead Pastor to assess our campus. Somehow, we had electricity... which was absolutely crazy, seeing as that most of our community did not. Just a few minutes after being on campus, the pastor's phone rang. One of our County Commissioners and County Sheriff Deputies were requesting if Church of Hope had power, and if so, if we would be willing to host a Special Needs Medical Shelter in dire need of power. These were patients who had nowhere to go and needed power for medical machinery to survive, and who needed a place to stay. Without hesitating, we said yes. And we had no idea what that week would entail.

As hundreds of special needs patients were transported to Church of Hope, volunteers showed up to help flip the campus into a hospital. It was incredible! As patients arrived, we quickly discovered what we needed to do—over the next few days, over 250 volunteers from across our community came, countless supplies were donated, every single meal was covered, and God took care of every need that arose. I had no idea what we were stepping into when we said yes, we just knew people were in crisis and they needed HOPE.

That week, as I manned "Hope Hospital Central" right here at this desk, physically, mentally, and emotionally I was tired. I didn't have power at my home, like countless others. I just wanted to take a really good shower. I didn't get a lot of sleep. Coffee was constantly in my hand. I was stretched leading an operation I could have never even imagined leading. But I kept going back to the foundation God breathed into my bones just a few days before He knew I would need it, and every morning I laced up my warrior boots with peace. In the face of tragedy, when I just wanted to cry, I remembered those who were searching for hope and didn't have a home to go to, and I paused, I smiled, I breathed more slowly, and I chose peace both for myself and to extend extra to those around me too.

Peace is a choice we make, not an external set of circumstances. When the crazy comes our way—and it will—walking in peace is no different. We don't feel our way into peace, we walk our way into peace.

Abigail didn't pause to think through her emotions, allow herself to get angry at her husband for being so dramatic and mean, or even think through the cost of giving away goods... she acted.

> "Now think it over and see what you can do, because disaster is hanging over our master and his whole household. He is such a wicked man that no one can talk to him."
> 18 Abigail acted quickly. She took two hundred loaves of bread, two skins of wine, five dressed sheep, five seahs of roasted grain, a hundred cakes of raisins and two hundred cakes of pressed figs, and loaded them on donkeys.
> 19 Then she told her servants, "Go on ahead; I'll follow you." But she did not tell her husband Nabal.
> 20 As she came riding her donkey into a mountain ravine, there were David and his men descending toward her, and she met them.
> 21 David had just said, "It's been useless—all my watching over this fellow's property in the wilderness so that nothing of his was missing. He has paid me back evil for good.
> 22 May God deal with David, be it ever so severely, if by morning I leave alive one male of all who belong to him!"
> 23 When Abigail saw David, she quickly got off her donkey and bowed down before David with her face to the

> ground. [24] She fell at his feet and said: "Pardon your servant, my lord, and let me speak to you; hear what your servant has to say." (1 Samuel 25:17-24, NIV)

Talk about an "un-peaceful" situation. Her husband chose to throw a power play at David, a man extending kindness, by reacting with anger and hatred. He stirred up chaos, not peace. As soon as Abigail got wind of what her husband had done, she didn't hesitate. She gathered supplies, laced up her warrior boots, and marched out to meet David. Her posture and actions screamed peace. And as a result, she ended up saving her family and friends.

Does your posture and do your actions scream peace?

Posture comes from what's happening inside us. It's the voices in our head, the words we speak to ourselves, the thoughts we allow to run rampant—what's in us is revealed by how we carry ourselves. A warrior woman walking in peace walks tall and confidently, even if everything around her is in distress, because she's choosing to walk grounded in peace.

Actions are how we choose to respond. When you see your friends had a GNO (Girls Night Out) without you; when your significant other picks a fight after a long day; when you get that call from your kid's principal's office for the third time this week; when your boss doesn't give you the raise you hoped for... when we want to retaliate in anger, a warrior woman walking in peace extends peace. She doesn't make a snarky remark to her friends; she doesn't fight back with her spouse trying to prove a point; she doesn't walk into the principal's office with a chip on her shoulder; she doesn't talk trash about her boss behind her back... she acts with peace.

Abigail acted in peace too—not just towards David, but toward her husband. Check out 1 Samuel 25:35-38 (NIV),

> [35] Then David accepted from her hand what she had brought him and said, "Go home in peace. I have heard your words and granted your request." [36] When Abigail went to Nabal, he was in the house holding a banquet like that of a king. He was in

> high spirits and very drunk. So she told him nothing at all until daybreak. [37] Then in the morning, when Nabal was sober, his wife told him all these things, and his heart failed him and he became like a stone. [38] About ten days later, the Lord struck Nabal and he died.

She had wisdom in when and how to approach her husband, and didn't pick a fight to show him just how wrong he was. She did her part and trusted God with the rest.

This doesn't mean peace is a passive, weak way of living. Quite the contrary. Peace is the strongest way you and I could ever live. Living in the posture and actions of peace is warrior work... it's not for the faint of heart.

Walking rooted in peace is a lot like taking a leap of faith. I had the privilege of participating in a leadership class with businessmen and women from across my community with our Ocala & Marion County Chamber & Economic Partnership, LOM Class XXXII (the best class ever!). On our third day as a group, we did a ropes course. One of our challenges was to literally take a leap of faith. We were each charged with climbing a huge pole, balancing on the top, and jumping off, reaching for and hopefully grabbing onto a bar in mid-air. We each eyed the challenge, nerves running rampant... would we be able to balance on top? Could we hang onto the bar? Was it even possible? How high up was it?

As each person climbed to the top and got their balance, every single one of us froze for a second, and the instructor below calmly reminded us to BREATHE. Take a breath. Just breathe. As I climbed and got my balance, looking at that bar, a flash of fear filled my mind... what if I couldn't grab it? What if I couldn't hold on? Panic and anxiety crept in, and I heard "Breathe!"

So, I breathed.
In. Out. In. Out.
And I jumped.

And here's the thing, I didn't hold onto the bar. But as my feet gently landed the ground I was so proud that I breathed through the panic and chose to jump. As I walked back towards the group, the instructor asked if anyone wanted to try again. Pieces of my mind screamed, "NO WAY EMILY! You don't have to prove anything... why go through that anxiety again?" But a larger part of myself wanted to see if I could push through the panic... and I really wanted to see if I could grab ahold of that bar!

I climbed, I paused, I breathed my way through, and before I took my leap of faith, I felt sheer peace as I latched onto that bar with every ounce of energy in me. I felt so proud of myself for fighting through the uncomfortable feelings inside my chest to have faith that I could do something hard. And I did it.

Warrior friend, this is what lacing up your warrior boots with peace looks like. It's taking a leap of faith. It's rooting everything in faith in someone you can't see, but who has your every step in His view. This is exactly what Abigail did—she took a leap, she gathered what she needed and marched onward, extending peace in the face of chaos.

How can we lace up our warrior boots in peace? This is the turning point, the ultimate peace game changer. There are tons of great strategies and tips for choosing peace—however, strategies won't last without the right foundation.

You see, I can put warrior boots on my feet, and I can walk around okay, but if I don't lace them up, I won't be able to run into battle when the chaos comes. I'll trip over my own two feet. To completely lace up your warrior boots with peace, you must go ALL IN and believe Peace is a Person we trust. Peace isn't the absence of problems, it's the presence of God.

Walking rooted in peace begins here, with Jesus. Jesus is peace. Without a personal relationship with Him, warrior friend, you could do all the self-help steps possible and perhaps experience a sense of peace for a day or a week, but it won't last apart from Peace Himself. It would be like attempting to walk around with untied warrior boots... you can take a step or two, but you won't be able to charge into battle in the long run.

Peace—and lacing up your warrior boots in peace—begins with a *relationship* with Peace.

> For to us a child is born, to us a son is given, and the government will be on his shoulders. And he will be called Wonderful Counselor, Mighty God, Everlasting Father, Prince of Peace.
> (Isaiah 9:6, NIV)

> For God is not a God of disorder but of peace—as in all the congregations of the Lord's people.
> (1 Corinthians 14:33, NIV)

> Now may the Lord of peace himself give you peace at all times and in every way. The Lord be with all of you.
> (2 Thessalonians 3:16, NIV)

> I have told you these things, so that in me you may have peace. In this world you will have trouble. But take heart! I have overcome the world.
> (John 16:33, NIV)

The God of the Universe sent His only Son to die for you and for me, offering eternal life and peace with Him forever. The only lasting peace you and I can ever experience! And the best part is, it's a free gift, we just have to choose to receive it.

If you've never accepted the gift of Peace Himself, today is your day! Romans 10:9 says, *"If you declare with your mouth, 'Jesus is Lord,' and believe in your heart that God raised him from the dead, you will be saved"* (NIV). Today, confess and believe. Invite Peace in. There's no magic formula or special words for inviting Jesus to be Lord of your life—use your own words or make this yours:

> *God, thank you for loving me. Thank you for sending Your son to die for me. I confess my sins and ask you to cleanse me, making me new. I invite you, Jesus, to be my Lord and Savior. Thank you for being my eternal Peace. Amen.*

If you just invited Jesus into your story, I am SO proud of you! Warrior friend, I'd love to celebrate with you. This is the most important decision you will ever make. I'd love to hear from you! Email me at emily@becomingme.tv.

It's time to walk rooted, lacing up your warrior boots in peace.

I can recognize
the painful stuff
without living there.

rocky road ice cream is a lot like life.

"Character cannot be developed in ease and quiet. Only through experience of trial and suffering can the soul be strengthened, ambition inspired, and success achieved."

- Helen Keller

Sweet and salty. Crisp. Gooey. Dripping with chocolate and overflowing with flavor. I've always characterized Rocky Road Ice Cream as a dessert with flavor, with spunk, with attitude. It's not soft and fluffy. It punches to the core, demands attention, and boldly proclaims, "I'm here!" with hidden surprises in every bite.

When I have rough days, I crave Rocky Road ice cream.

Maybe it's because the rich sweetness and texture awaken my senses—while giving me the permission to drown my sorrows in a tub of ice cream. But mostly, when I eat Rocky Road, I'm reminded that life, too, is rocky. It's full of soft marshmallow-y days and rigid almond-fortress kinda days. But when you mix the two together, something magical happens, something extraordinary takes place.

The melting pot days of crunchy soft are often—when we look back—the most delicious. Those days your to-do list seems insurmountable and you find an encouraging note from a friend in the mailbox; one relational chapter runs its course and a new one flourishes over a Starbucks vanilla latte; you discover your finances aren't where they need to be but then develop a spreadsheet system the accountant at work would drool over; someone criticizes your work and you receive a Twitter DM about how you're making a difference in the life of someone you don't know that well.

Life is a mixture of the sugar-coated celebrations and bawl-your-eyes-out thunderstorms. And we need both to make it the grand adventure that it is. It seems like a contradiction of sorts, but the two go together, hand-in-hand creating this yummy concoction called life.

On the days you find me eating Rocky Road straight out of the carton, it's because I'm reminding myself that I need both the marshmallow-y and almond-y moments in order to become the woman God made me to be. My natural instinct is to see the rough and rigid circumstances at a level so magnified that the sweet and savory instances get lost. And that's not okay with me. I want my life to be rich in flavor, rich in gumption, and rich in celebration. I want to celebrate—to magnify—the moments Jesus is tangibly reaching down and saying, "Baby girl, I love you. Your story's not over yet," and I want to recognize the painful stuff without living there.

Life's a Rocky Road, friends. The question is: will we embrace all of the ingredients, savoring the sweet and appreciating the lessons learned in the rougher terrain? Or will the rocky patches drown out the good stuff, leaving us in a depressing pile of almonds?

This girl's grabbing a spoon and digging into the crunchy soft. Who's with me?

becoming's a marathon, not a sprint.

"A strong woman looks a challenge dead in the eye and gives it a wink."

- Anonymous

My first half marathon took place in sunny Orlando, Florida, with three of my running buddies from high school and college. We trained for months. We conquered the early Saturday morning habit and knew the back roads of our little town like the backs of our hands. We'd gone through old shoes, lots of sticky, humid miles, and hundreds of songs on our running playlists. We were ready. We came to conquer. And we had a finishing goal at the forefront of our minds: break the two-hour mark. In our minds, finishing at 1:50:00 would be ideal, but optimistically, we aimed to come in anywhere under 2:00:00.

Race day came. Humidity was high and the sun was ready to shine brightly on the course. The four of us started strong and kept a steady, comfortable, yet speedy pace for the first 10 miles. We sang, we cheered each other on, we were all smiles.

And then I got sick.

My stomach began doing summersaults as I felt the panicky feelings of nausea coming quickly. I told my friends to run ahead so I could catch my breath and promised I would catch up to them.

My last three miles was an uphill battle. Willing myself to put one foot in front of the other was the only thing on my mind. Finish, finish, finish. Catch up to my friends. Finish.

I jogged the last mile as best as I could and crossed that finish line at 2:03:22. I remember seeing my family, cheering loudly, ready to congratulate me as I crossed the finish line. But I wasn't happy. My last three miles left me so frustrated that I couldn't enjoy the finish. I hurried across the finish line, paused for pictures, but then, rather than wanting to celebrate with my friends, I just wanted to leave. I wanted to hop in the car, go home, puke and sulk.

Fast-foward to half marathon number two on the colorful Las Vegas Strip. While living in Las Vegas, running the Rock 'N' Roll Half Marathon had been at the top of my bucket list, so I grabbed a few friends, signed up, and began training. This time around, my training looked much different than my prep time for the Orlando Half Marathon. My running was more sporadic than I had hoped, my times were off, my body was still adjusting to the dryness of the desert, and as race day approached, I was physically nowhere near as ready as I had been only a year earlier for my first half marathon.

But, I laced up my shoes, met my running group, and lined up with the other runners assigned to my corral. I started with low expectations and was simply ready to have fun running the Strip at night. It was electrifying. The lights shimmered and we were greeted with DJs, spectators, and music at almost every turn. As I ran, I couldn't help but smile, seeing this city I had moved across the country to in a different way.

As we neared mile 10, my nerves began to shake—would I get sick again? Would my body react? We ran past mile 10, past mile 11, past mile 12 and as we neared the finish line, my adrenaline set in—I was doing this. And I was finishing strong. Crossing that finish line, I felt like I could have kept going, could have kept running the race.

My finish time was nowhere near my first half marathon, but how I felt at the finish line was completely different—I was ecstatic.

I ran the same distance in both of those races, but my finish was entirely different. I can't help but think the same is true in life.

> Let us strip off every weight that slows us down, especially the sin that so easily trips us up. And let us run with endurance the race God has set before us. [2] We do this by keeping our eyes on Jesus, the champion who initiates and perfects our faith. Because of the joy awaiting Him, He endured the cross, disregarding its shame. Now He is seated in the place of honor beside God's throne. (Hebrews 12:1-2, NLT)

The hardest part of both of my half marathons were the last three miles. The vast majority of the race was well behind me and the finish line was so close I could taste it. But, I still had three miles to go. The race wasn't over just yet. And it was here, in those last few miles, that I had a choice to make: would I finish strong, would I coast by simply "finishing to finish," or would I hit a wall and give up entirely?

My Daddy shared this incredible truth with me surrounding this idea of finishing well: "The enemy doesn't fight you for where you are. He fights you for where you're going." How we decide to finish makes all the difference.

Perhaps you're finishing a season or certain chapter of life. Maybe a relationship you thought was headed towards marriage is coming to an end; perhaps you're transitioning between jobs; maybe it's time to pack your bags and move to a new city; perhaps you're close to wrapping up a massive project at work; or maybe you're almost at the end of your pregnancy, ready to welcome new life to this world.

Wherever you are today, keep running... one step at a time. Finishing strong is the best way to start what's next. How we run the last three miles is entirely up to us. We can either lean into the panic of past experiences and pull up short, or forge onward, pushing past the fear of the unknown and trusting God with each next step, giving it our very best.

What kind of runner will you choose to be today?

moving forward after a break-up.

"It always seems impossible until it's done."

- Nelson Mandela

It was the perfect fall night in Vegas. A cool breeze rippled across the desert mountains just beckoning me to go for a night run. I texted my running partner, we quickly laced up our running shoes, and met at our favorite spot.

This wasn't our first run at this particular park. In fact, this was our usual meeting place. We knew the course well and knew how to navigate the trail in the dark. We soon found a sweet rhythm and fell into comfortable conversation. Along the way, the light posts on the trail grew dim. To shed light on the rocky path in front of us, I flipped on my phone flashlight so we wouldn't miss a beat.

Splat!

In a split-second, my body hit the ground and skidded across the rocks. My right hand gripped my phone while my left hand tried to halt my forward velocity. I pushed myself to my feet and started running again. My running partner quickly asked if I was okay, and I prompted us to simply continue on the trail. Feeling no instant pain, I began thinking everything was probably alright.

And then I felt the blood trickling down into my socks by my ankles. Trying to shake it off, I kept running until the pain began pounding like a constant, annoying knock on your front door while you're trying to take a nap. Constant, pounding, aching.

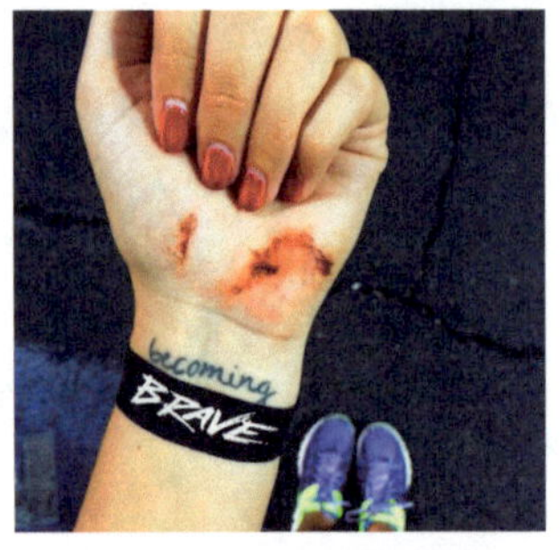

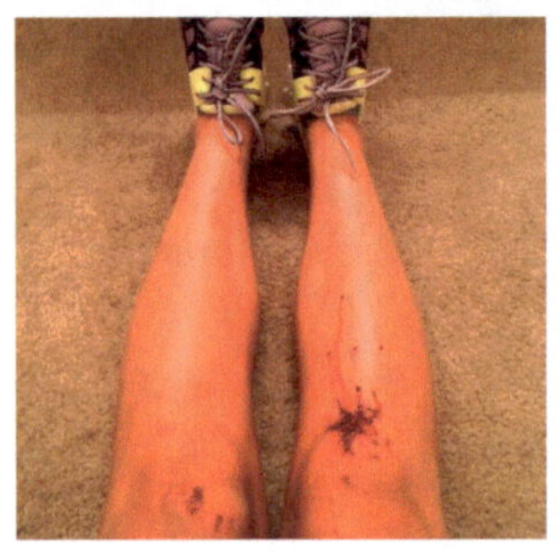

We ran to the nearest light post and I instantly saw that my hands and knees were not okay. Raw skin hung off my legs and blood oozed out of my open wounds. We finished running, I poured water down my legs and picked up bandages from the nearest store. Gingerly cleaning my bloody knees, I carefully tried to remove dirt and find a comfortable way to sleep through the night without agitating my wounds.

The next day, I grabbed a handful of bandages and knew jeans weren't an option. My legs wouldn't stop bleeding so I sported a skirt for work, bandaged my knees and went on my way. As I drove to the office, I called my Daddy to talk through the events of the night. He asked a slew of questions and shared something that would later impact me on a much deeper level than my bleeding, wounded knees.

He said, "Emily, you need to go home, turn on your shower head to the hardest setting it will operate on and you need to scrub your wounds. You need to clean out the excess rocks and dirt. Baby, it's going to hurt. It's going to sting and it's not going to be fun. But if you don't do this, you could get an infection and then a doctor would have to open your closed wounds and scrape out the debris. Take the time to thoroughly clean out your wounds."

I listened. I turned my car around and took the most painful shower I've ever experienced in my life. But as I stepped out of the pain, out of that shower, I knew my Daddy was right. If I hadn't taken the time to really clean my wounds, I probably would have had a much bigger problem down the road.

Break-ups feel like bloody knee moments in life—one moment your relationship is moving forward and then *splat!*, in the next moment you feel the immediate force of a complete break, and find yourself left to assess the damage.

We don't walk into dating relationships already anticipating breaking up. We say yes to one date and the next and the next because we like doing life with that person, and then we can't imagine our story without them written in it. Whether you find yourself doing the breaking up or being broken up with, the shock still stings. You wake up the next day, fingers twitching to text that familiar person, and achingly realize that person's not in your story anymore. Relational break ups hurt, they leave a mark. They leave our emotions bloodied and bruised, dirt and debris clinging to the chambers of our hearts. We attempt to dust ourselves off, bandage our wounds, do everything in our power to stop the bleeding, and gradually watch the gnarly wreckage of baggage build up inside of us.

But here's the thing—it's not our wounds that define us, it's what we do after we're injured that matters. By leaving debris in the opening of my pain, I only make my hurt worse—I don't allow myself to actually heal from my relational break-up. I'm simply masking an open sore, pretending everything is okay, when in reality, it's not. How I choose to clean out my wounded heart matters.

In the midst of the healing process, how can we scrub and clean out our wounds?

Identify your pain and grieve the loss. Grab a journal, a trusted friend, or a counselor, and name your pain. Walk through the break-up.

moving forward after a break-up.

Ask questions. How did it make you feel? Why did it make you feel that way? Work through the deep, gritty places to identify the root of your pain. We can't clean out our wounds if we don't know where they are. Take the time to identify the core issues so you can discover lasting healing.

Clean house. What physical reminders do you have from the person, place, circumstance or situation that left you with bloody knees? Delete text messages, emails and Facebook messages; unfollow on social media; throw away letters; pack up a box of clothes or tokens and take it to a thrift store; throw away and delete photos. To heal, we must remove the dirt, the grime, the muck, the hurt. I get it, this may seem harsh, but warrior friend... I've been here. You can't heal without cleaning out your wound.

Give yourself time. Just like physical wounds take time to heal, our hearts also need time to heal. Initially, we'll make it through the steps of identifying pain, asking the tough questions and cleaning house, and will still feel the sting of the pain. That's normal. It's a part of the healing process. Healing will hurt, but it leaves you stronger. We can never undo what has been done to us, but we are never broken, only bruised.

Stand your ground. It would be silly for me to thoroughly clean out my bloody knees, allow them to heal, and then cut them back open... right? The same is true with the pain we experience in life. After taking the time to truly heal, don't cut your wounds back open. Don't go back to places of pain, or hurt.

My knees and hands are now adorned with some pretty gnarly scars from that eventful fall night. But you know what? Those bumpy, rough patches of skin don't make me grimace like they used to. They aren't causing physical pain. They're simply there, a part of me, a part of who I'm becoming.

The same is true for those places of healing in my heart. I have scars from broken relationships, unmet expectations, betrayed trust, disappointment, shame, unhealthy decisions, and rejection. But those scars are simply scars. They aren't oozing pain anymore because I scrubbed my wounds, and I cleaned out my heart from the muck that was fighting to take up permanent residence inside. Fighting for healing became one of the sweetest gifts on my becoming journey.

My scars don't define me. My scars don't dictate my future. They simply remind me of God's presence in the storm and His promise to never leave me or forsake me. My scars remind me of the incredible hope I have in Jesus. They leave me so thankful for a Savior whose body was beaten, bruised and ridden with scars born out of deep, abiding, never-changing love for me. My scars remind me of love, of acceptance, and of the truth that I have not been rejected.

Warrior friend, the pain you're feeling doesn't define you or your becoming story. It's just a chapter. But don't stay stuck in this chapter. Pick yourself up, lace up your warrior boots and do the hard work, the warrior work. Clean out the deepest points of your hurt and fix your eyes unwaveringly on the hope we have in Christ. This break up doesn't define you. Perhaps it's God's sweetest gift, protecting you for His very best that you just haven't met yet.

what happens when we allow the evil in the world to become the evil in us?

"I can't change the direction of the wind, but I can adjust my sails to always reach my destination."

- Jimmy Dean

Robert Frost once wisely reflected, "Two roads diverged in a yellow wood, and sorry I could not travel both and be one traveler, long I stood and looked down one as far as I could to where it bent in the undergrowth." The poem continues with Frost choosing the road less traveled, ending with the famous line, "Two roads diverged in a wood, and I—I took the one less traveled by, and that has made all the difference."

I was standing in my own yellow wood of sorts, torn between the road of redemption and the road of bitterness. My trust had been violated. Someone I cared deeply about—a friend who I thought had my back—broke my trust. What do you do when your trust is broken?

The classic character from Sleeping Beauty, Maleficent, knows a thing or two about betrayal, shame, grace and redemption. Known as a fairytale villain, Maleficent lived a misunderstood tale. The namesake 2014 Disney movie revealed the narrative untold—the story of the woman scorned, playing the role of both her own villain and hero.

Maleficent lived a magical life. She loved deeply and, in turn, was hurt deeply. One ominous night, the man she loved seduced her and ripped the most precious thing from her body: her wings. Maleficent's screams and scars reflect a woman battered and bruised, a woman at the crossroads of a yellow wood of her own.

Maleficent had a choice to make: would she allow that which was stolen from her to define her? Or would it make her stronger? Initially, she chose the path of the woman scorned. And don't we know this stance? We can spot her from a mile away. She walked with extreme fury, a force to be reckoned with, a woman to be feared. She built a fearsome wall of thorns, literally blocking out anything and anyone that could pose the potential threat of hurting her again. Her motto had become, "Hurt me once, shame on you. Hurt me twice, shame on me." Maleficent lived so blinded by her own pain that she cursed the very person that held the keys to a different kind of story—a story of redemption.

Here's the thing that I love about Maleficent's story: she didn't stay there. Initially she chose the path of revenge, but she resolved that she didn't want to live there. The movie reflects "she reveled in the sorrow her curse had brought."

What she deemed as the ultimate vengeance became bitter ashes to her own heart. As she sought to set that which she had cursed right, she grievously reflected, "I was so lost in hatred and revenge." Maleficent lost herself when she chose to walk down the trail of revenge, bitterness and destruction. She had allowed the evil in the world to become the evil in her.

As I contemplate the two roads before me, I'm drawing from Maleficent's story and asking myself a few questions:

1. What will my pain turn me into? A monster? A woman to be feared? Bitter? Or will the pain make me better, stronger and steep my story in grace?
2. Who will I invite to be my wings when I don't have any? Who will be that person speaking into me providing perspective when I can't see clearly?
3. What lies beyond my own fearsome wall of thorns?
4. Perhaps, could that person/thing/circumstance that I have cursed be the very key to unlocking my own redemption story?
5. What step(s) do I need to take to begin walking the road of redemption?

The road of redemption isn't about—and never was about—the person that betrayed and hurt me. This road is about me and my story. It's about my own health, sanity, peace of mind, and being the warrior God created me to be. God never designed us to merely survive; He made us to thrive. Here's what I know to be true: I can be the warrior or the villain in my story... but I can't be both. That person who let me down, well, my story doesn't end with them. They're simply a footnote in a chapter of my life. They won't define my story because I'm choosing the road of the warrior, not the villain. The road of redemption, not revenge.

> So, what do you think? With God on our side like this, how can we lose? If God didn't hesitate to put everything on the line for us, embracing our condition and exposing himself to the worst by sending his own Son, is there anything else he wouldn't gladly and freely do for us? And who would dare tangle with God by messing with one of God's chosen? Who would dare even to point a finger? The One who died for us—who was raised to life for us!—is in the presence of God at this very moment

> sticking up for us. Do you think anyone is going to be able to drive a wedge between us and Christ's love for us? There is no way! Not trouble, not hard times, not hatred, not hunger, not homelessness, not bullying threats, not backstabbing, not even the worst sins listed in Scripture: They kill us in cold blood because they hate you. We're sitting ducks; they pick us off one by one. None of this fazes us because Jesus loves us. I'm absolutely convinced that nothing—nothing living or dead, angelic or demonic, today or tomorrow, high or low, thinkable or unthinkable—absolutely nothing can get between us and God's love because of the way that Jesus our Master has embraced us.
> (Romans 8:31-39, MSG)

Look what hurt you in the face and say, "IT'S OVER." That thing, person or circumstance will attempt to grip onto you for dear life, but in order to step onto the road less traveled we have to let the hurt, pain, betrayal, heartache, and unmet expectations go. When we allow the evil in the world to become the evil in us, we stop being who God created us to be. And that road isn't worth it. So warrior friend, stand up, unlock the cage around your heart, grab my hand, and together let's walk down the road of redemption. Are you ready?

when it feels like you're the only single person in the world.

"Don't try to find the right person... BE the right person."
- Mark Cummins

One Halloween, I found myself straight ugly crying while stuffing bread in my face. Yes, this was me. I'd spiraled into the mental lie that threatens to isolate us, keeping us from being who God made us to be: *you are the only one in the world experiencing this.*

It's so easy to get caught in the six inches between your ears, creating false realities in your mind. On this particular day, my false reality was that I was the only single person in the world. As I sat at my parent's kitchen counter, eating honey glazed dinner rolls while sobbing so hard it was almost impossible to understand what I was even saying, I complained: "Mom! I am literally the only single person of all my friends. I must be the only single person in the entire world... I'm never going to get married!"

Insert dramatic face palm here

when it feels like you're the only single person in the world.

My Mom with a soft but tough love, looked me straight in the eyes and challenged me: "Emily, you are not the only single person in the world," after which she began listing friends and family who were unmarried too. I know, I know... come on, Emily. It's ridiculous to believe I am the *only* single person *in the entire world*. Duh. But that wasn't the root issue that day... it was just the lie inviting me into isolation.

My Mom continued, "Have you asked God if you're going to get married?" Well... that one stopped me in my tracks. In-between bites, I mustered, "Mom... duh. Of course I've asked God that question. But He hasn't done anything about it lately while all my friends are getting married!" Without hesitating, she pushed back: "Emily, if God told you He has a man for you, why are you so worked up? Do you trust Him?"

Do you trust Him?

At first, her questioning just made me mad. I mean, of course I had talked to God and asked Him if marriage was a part of my story... or had I? As I really stopped and considered my Mom's words, I realized that in all my talking at God about wanting a relationship and seeing Him move in the relationship department in other's lives and not mine, I hadn't slowed down enough to ask *Him* whether that was even a chapter He was going to write in my story. So I put my buttery dinner rolls down and began a conversation with the Bread of Life Himself.

When I walk down the path of believing I am the only person in the world experiencing something—whether that's singleness, health issues, friendship break-ups, really tough projects at work, financial stress, or anything!—I'm leaning into the exact lie the enemy wants me to believe: that I am alone. And warrior friend, you and I are far from alone. Because I have a relationship with Jesus Christ, I am never alone. He is with me, He is in me, and He is for me. Stepping into isolation causes me to move my eyes away from trusting Him and onto me... what I can control and do. My Pastor and Daddy, said this recently: "When you decide to take matters in your own hands, you look down and see that what you get is in your own hands... not God's." The dangerous tight rope I walked that October night was taking matters into my own hands—and, in turn, risking forfeiting all that God has promised me.

Ouch.

It didn't take me long to realize just how right my Mom was. I talked to God, heard His voice, and knew my pity party needed to come to a quick end. So I wiped the tears from my face, thanked God for answering my prayer, and laced up my warrior boots... literally. It was Halloween, right? So I suited up in my Wonder Woman costume and invited the Wonder Woman within to breathe again... trusting that the God who created her knows best for her, has a plan for her, and that if He has promised something, He will surely deliver.

> Promise me, O women of Jerusalem, not to awaken love until the time is right.
> (Song of Solomon 8:4, NLT)

It would be easy today to slip into the shadows of isolation. Scrolling through Instagram the week of Valentine's Day when you're single can feel... very anticlimactic. That wise man who spoke about taking matters into your own hands? He also said this: "Who you are in God matters most... you've got to have a healthy me before there can be a healthy we. God is championing something in you. Will you live fully satisfied in God and trust Him for 'someone'? God is the expert on romance."

This is my challenge to me, and my challenge to us: will you believe that God is the expert on romance? That God is the expert on your story? And that the story He is writing is so much better than you could ever imagine?

No... you are not the only single person in the world. And if you were, would it even matter? Because the last time I checked, my God is still the God of miracles—do I trust Him enough that even if I was the only single person in the world, He would still show up for me as He promised?

> Trust in the Lord with all your heart; do not depend on your own understanding. [6] Seek his will in all you do, and he will show you which path to take. [7] Don't be impressed with your own wisdom. Instead, fear the Lord and turn away from evil. Then you will have healing for your body and strength for your bones.
> (Proverbs 3:5-8, NLT)

Warrior friend, God surely is the expert on romance. Do you believe it? Do you trust Him? When lies of isolation creep in, will you choose to run... not walk... straight to the Bread of Life and live fully satisfied in Him?

dear future husband.

"You write a beautiful story. From glory to glory, I believe."
- "Beautiful Story", by the Belonging Co.

I don't know your name.
I don't know what your hair color is or what makes you smile.
I don't know what makes you laugh until you cry.
I don't know what your dreams are or what your deepest fears are.
I don't know what your favorite food is.
I don't know what irritates you or makes you angry.
I don't know the sound of your laugh or if you're a country music kinda guy.
I don't know you.
I don't know you, but I feel like I do.

Because here's what I do know:
I know you love Jesus with every fiber in your being.
I know you're chasing after becoming the man God created you to be.
I know you're not perfect.

I know you'll never complete me because no human ever will.
I know you'll be my biggest cheerleader in my own becoming journey.

With what I know about you and the man you're becoming—and what I know about me and the woman I'm becoming—here's my prayer, my commitment, my promise:
I will wait for you.
I will pray for you daily.
I will cheer you on, encourage and support you.
I won't compete with you, but will complement you.
I will love you fully, passionately and unconditionally.
When the tough stuff comes—and it will—I won't give up or quit.
I won't be perfect because I'm human, but I'll bring my best every day.

You know what I believe to be true? We are both becoming; discovering who we are and who we want to be. We're waking up to what it is that God made us for, the passions He birthed inside us, the voice He gave to each of us. And I believe that we're going to be a good team, in the right time. When we're ready. When our stories are woven together to create something stronger, something bigger than anything we could ever attempt to accomplish on our own.

Song of Solomon 8:4 says, *"Don't excite love, don't stir it up, until the time is ripe—and you're ready"* (MSG). I don't know you, but I know the beat of your heart. And I'm not going to rush it. I'm not going to wish for a faster timetable or speed up the process. Because I value you more than that. I value who you're becoming in the process. And I value who I'm becoming in the process, too. Until we meet, know this: a girl named Emily already loves you so, so much.

fighting to become you.

"In Christ, we fight from victory, not for victory."
- Mark Cummins

We all fight for something—whether it be fighting for good grades, physical health, strong relationships, career goals, or financial success. Culture preaches we must fight to prove validation, arguing that when we reach certain milestones, followers on social media, and accolades, then we will be deemed successful... we will have arrived.

But what if we have it all wrong?
What if in fighting for something, we're actually losing?
What if victory was actually fighting *from* something else entirely?

In the span of four verses in 2 Kings 5, we read about a young girl taken captive and thrust into the chains of slavery. This girl had everything taken from her—her freedom, her country, her family, her childhood. Yet, in a singular moment, she chose a different stance to fight from...

> Now bands of raiders from Aram had gone out and had taken captive a young girl from Israel, and she served Namaan's wife. [3] She said to her mistress, "If only my master would see the prophet who is in Samaria! He would cure him of his leprosy." [4] Namaan went to his master and told him what the girl from Israel had said. [5] "By all means, go," the king of Aram replied. "I will send a letter to the king of Israel."
>
> (2 Kings 5:2-5, NIV)

We're not given a timeline between verse 2 and verse 3; however, I am convicted by the posture this young girl takes. From the outside looking in, she has lost everything—she's kidnapped, taken to a foreign land, forced into slavery, and even her very name remains unspoken. Her childhood was stolen from her, her freedom vanquished, and her friends and family left behind. As she wakes up in her new world, we don't find a weak, heartbroken, shattered little girl. We find a warrior standing grounded regardless of the punches life threw at her.

She could have fought *for*...
Her freedom.
Her country.
Her family.
Her childhood.
Her name.

She could have fought *against*, throwing punches at...
Her masters.
The foreign land she found herself in.
Her new position.
Her master's illness.

Instead, she fought from the victory she knew she already had in Jesus Christ. She served out of her heart, knowing who she is and Whose she is. Rather than viewing her new life as a setback, she stepped in to the set-up from her God to invite people into His story, by offering a solution to her master's leprousy.

She fought *from*...
Her identity in God.
The truth of who she is in God.
The reality that no circumstance or person could ever take her identity away from her.

I find myself wondering what I would have done in her shoes. Would I have shrunk back in despair, doubting and questioning *why* God would have allowed this nightmare to be written into the threads of my story? Would I have shuffled my feet, passively aggressively serving my captors? Would I have lashed out in anger? Or, like this young woman, would I have chosen an eternal perspective, lacing up my warrior boots in the peace of God, choosing to be who He created me to be, for such a time as this?

When we know who we are and Whose we are, we fight from a different posture. We fight from the stance of the victory we already claim. Of everything in this world, there is *one thing* no one can take from you: your identity. Circumstances and people can change—you can have friends one day, and they can be gone the next; you can be on top of the world in your career one day, and packing a cardboard box with your office remnants the next; one day, you can be saying "I do" vowing to love that person forever, and watching them walk out the door spewing hateful words the next; one day you can have a clean bill of health, and the next receive a phone call from your doctor you never saw coming. We can't control what happens around us; we can control who we are and how we respond.

This is what the warrior in 2 Kings 5 understood. While everything she knew and loved was ripped away from her, she saw the most important thing could never be taken away—her identity as a daughter of God. The same is true for us.

My story woven throughout these pages is a testament to this very truth. When I moved from Las Vegas, launching my company in Florida, I wrapped my identity in being an entrepreneur. I thought that by labeling myself a "Girl Boss," I would have fought for victory and won, that I would have arrived as a success. The reality was God didn't design me to be an entrepreneur; He created me to be a minister and a pastor. It was only when I shut down my business and stepped into who He uniquely designed me to be, that I stood firm, balanced, able to take the punches life threw at me, because I was finally fighting from the victory I already had in Jesus Christ—my true identity as His daughter. I was no longer pretending to be someone I wasn't; I was no longer fighting to prove validation, or fighting against the people and circumstances around me. I was fighting to become who God made me to be from the victory that was mine to claim all along.

Romans 10 in The Message unpacks this posture for us:

> You're not "doing" anything; you're simply calling out to God, trusting Him to do it for you. That's salvation. With your whole being you embrace God setting things right, and then you say it, right out loud: "God has set everything right between Him and me!" Scripture reassures us, "No one who trusts God like this—heart and soul—will ever regret it."
>
> (Romans 10:8-10, MSG)

When I asked Jesus to forgive me of my sins and be my Savior, I entered into relationship with Him. It was there that He clothed me in a new identity no one can ever strip me of. I don't have to "do" anything; the beautiful thing about my God is that He has already won. He fights for me, and warrior friend, He fights for you, too.

What are you fighting for? What are you fighting from? What are you trying so desperately to prove to the world around you? Today is the day to release the posture of a failed fighter, and step into the ring ready to claim the victory that is already yours. John 1:12 says, *"To all who did receive Him, to those who believed in His Name, He gave the right to become children of God"* (NIV). Step into relationship with Him and claim your inheritance, identity, and victory as His child.

The only way you'll ever truly become who God made you to be is when you fight from victory, not for victory. You have nothing to prove. He has already proven it on the cross. Now, it's our decision to receive that gift of victory, to stamp on our hearts our identity as His daughters, and to fight each and every day to become who He made us to be from His victory alone.

becoming amanda.

This chapter was written by a fellow warrior with you in mind.

From the age of five to nineteen, I felt the Lord's direction for my life leading me to the ocean. Running hard for what felt like my life's purpose, I pursued a career in marine biology. And there, smack in the middle of that pursuit, I felt the Holy Spirit urgently prompt me to pivot towards a life of full-time ministry. I knew this would mean leaving behind everything I had worked towards, but trusting His plan, I took a leap of faith. I made a hard left and soon found myself on staff at a local church for seven years.

During those years, I thought I had traded my dreams for this "forever calling". I felt I had made my own big faith pivot that stories I admired were anchored on.

You may have a defining starting over moment in this life, too. If you're on the brink of one now, write this down where you can see it until you internalize it: **God isn't afraid of Genesis.**

Genesis. Where the Holy Spirit hovered over the vastness of nothing and God began to speak and subsequently bring everything we know and marvel at into existence. Creating a good thing from nothing is in His nature. That should infuse you and me with courage when we stand on the edge of everything we have known and gotten comfortable in and there is nothing that we can see in front of us. Genesis moments are the birthplace of audacious faith and riveting stories.

When I first met Emily, I was just on the other side of my step into full time ministry. And as I shared my own becoming story, my story felt complete. "I had this one life, now I have a different one. The Lord asked me to leave my nets like Peter and follow Him, so I did. Now I do this and that, and it's all just doused in this rich purpose I know the Lord had for me..." This was it. For life, right?

Imagine my surprise when I heard a rustle in the trees of the camp I called my everyday life, years into my "forever calling". It was the same Holy Spirit blowing through, with new instruction and that same pressing I had felt in college.

This one shook me. Would God ask me to start over again? On the other side, I can say: absolutely. The same God asking me to follow His lead again knows me, knows my past, holds my future, and has a plan. I reminded myself on the edge of yet another Genesis moment that I can trust Him. And so can you.

As I write this now, I have closed that chapter and opened several new ones. My fiance has become my husband and we have a wonderful, beautiful marriage. I started a business helping people with my swiss army knife of skills. And now, my husband and I are about to embark on a completely new and uncharted holy plot twist as we prepare to relocate together at the Lord's lead. Once again, starting afresh with this life, our community, and adding another layer onto who we are each becoming.

I've held plenty of roles in my life that just don't follow any kind of pattern or make sense by the world's terms. I've been a student of science and the owner of a creative business. I've been a waitress, a writer, an engineer, an event planner... I've taught graphic design, and I've taught pre-algebra. I've been on platforms and in boardrooms and behind cubicles and in literal quicksand up to my knees. And in it all, there's still one constant theme.

Like Paul said in Philippians 4:11, "I have learned to be content in whatever circumstances I find myself." I am arguably not as quick to it as Paul, but after I sit in the shift awhile, I find the Lord's presence or purpose has never left me. This is the common thread that runs through my story with its many ever-changing nuances.

I am one of a hundred thousand stories that prove it's okay, rather advantageous actually, to follow more than one set path in your life. We are conditioned to pick "our thing" in this life and stick it out no matter what, lest we sacrifice security or success. But that is just not always the way life plays out when we intend to walk by the Spirit of God and yield our lives to His direction and His timing.

The good news is that there is nothing wasted when the Lord is in our stories. The entirety of the collection of your lived experiences—and the ones yet you come—play into who you have become and who you are becoming. They are all critical, valuable, and nonexclusive.

We leave none in the past, completely. Rather, they lay like brick upon brick as our character, expertise, competency, and—as Loki would say—our "glorious purpose" when we place them all on the foundation that is Jesus Christ and His magnificent, personal sovereignty.

My prayer for you is that you choose to be a woman who leans into the adventure of a lifetime. Choose to be a woman content with being undefined by the average standard. Choose to not discount your past experiences because they are so valuable to who you are today. Choose to say "yes" to God, even if it means walking away from everything He's led you to this far.

Each time I look back at my own story, and especially on the backdrop of God's hand in Genesis, this has been a steadfast truth: When God creates, it is good.

warrior steps.

(1) What are some of your favorite warrior stories? What about how these warriors live inspires you? Will you choose to be the warrior God designed you to be?

(2) What does it mean for you to lace up your warrior boots in peace?

(3) How will you choose to embrace the "rocky road" of life?

(4) What kind of runner will you choose to be in your becoming story? Will you finish strong, or give up?

(5) What step(s) do you need to take today to heal, scrub and clean out your wounds?

(6) Will you commit to looking what hurt you in the face and say, "IT'S OVER"? When we allow the evil in the world to become the evil in us, we stop being who God created us to be. Will you choose to walk down the road of redemption?

(7) Do you believe God is the expert on romance? Do you trust Him? Spend time talking with Him about your thoughts on romance and relationships today.

(8) To my single warrior friends, write a letter to your future husband. To my married warrior friends, write a letter to your husband.

(9) What are you fighting for? What are you fighting from? What are you trying so desperately to prove to the world around you? Today is the day to release the posture of a failed fighter, and to step into the ring ready to claim the victory that is already yours. Write John 1:12 on a sticky note and put it where you'll see it daily, reminding you that in Christ we fight FROM victory, not FOR victory.

fail + fly.

"Love who you are, but love who you're becoming more."
- Autumn Calabrese

more being, less doing.

"The only person you are destined to become is the person you decide to be."

- Ralph Waldo Emerson

One morning before heading into a busy day of meetings, deadlines and endless cups of coffee, I was struck with a question that completely wrecked me: *When did my love for Jesus lose its vigor?*

As I began to dive into that question, several others began flooding to the surface as well: *Did I begin equating what I was doing with my love for God? Why hadn't I been spending consistent time with Jesus? How could I change that?*

Doing does not equal a relationship.
Doing does not equal knowing.
Doing does not equal intimacy.
Doing does not equal love.

Instantly the story of two sisters in Luke 10 came to the forefront of my mind. Mary and Martha were contrasted in how they went about their relationship with Jesus—Mary sat with Jesus in awe, while Martha was consumed with accomplishing tasks for Jesus. Both women were in His presence, both women knew Him, yet only one was acting in relationship with Jesus.

> As Jesus and His disciples were on their way, He came to a village
> where a woman named Martha opened her home to him. 39 She
> had a sister called Mary, who sat at the Lord's feet listening to
> what He said. 40 But Martha was distracted by all the preparations
> that had to be made. She came to Him and asked, "Lord, don't
> you care that my sister has left me to do the work by myself? Tell
> her to help me!"
> 41 "Martha, Martha," the Lord answered, "you are worried and
> upset about many things, 42 but few things are needed—or indeed
> only one. Mary has chosen what is better, and it will not be taken
> away from her"
> (Luke 10:38-42, NIV).

While Martha scurried to check everything off of her checklist, she ignored Jesus, missing out on spending time in His presence, missing out on enjoying her relationship with Him. Mary, on the other hand, set everything aside. She had one, singular focus: to know Jesus. Period. She wasn't worried about "doing" for Him, she prioritized getting to know Him.

You know what I discovered? I had picked up my Martha mindset and set aside my Mary heart. And that's a dangerous place to be. That's not a place I want to take up permanent residence in. That's not who I want to be or the posture I want to embrace. I don't want to be so caught up in doing for Jesus that I miss getting to know Him entirely.

I'm beginning to see that the level of my passion for Jesus is rooted in the posture of my heart and my mindset. When my mindset begins tipping towards simply doing and overpowers my heart for knowing, everything gets off balance.

How can we trade our Martha mindsets for Mary hearts?

Get back to the basics. Set your alarm clock. Download the YouVersion Bible App and read a devotional plan. Read a chapter in Proverbs. Journal your prayers. Sing your favorite worship song. Go on an adventure outside. Simply put: get in His presence.

Probe the murky areas of your heart. What has you tangled up in knots? What are you worried about? What are you stressed over? What is keeping you awake at night? Identify those trigger points and clean your system. Get in the trenches, journal, talk with a trusted advisor, and take those areas into the presence of Jesus. Breathe out the muck, inhale His peace.

Identify your Nos. What do you need to say "no" to in order to say "yes" to unrushed time with Jesus? In saying "no," we ultimately are setting aside our Martha mindset and preparing to embrace our Mary heart.

It's time to get things back in order. It's time to, like Mary, set everything aside and sit at the feet of Jesus. It's time to live in "being," and not so much "doing." It's time.

What do you need to do today to lay down your Martha mindset and embrace your Mary heart? It's time, warrior friend.

I'm simply choosing the best yes for me.

the car jam session that checked my heart

"Renew your mind for a better next time."

- Mark Cummins

Lately, I've noticed how desensitized I've become to things I never thought I would have been comfortable with.

One December, I was cruising around town with my Daddy while I was home for Christmas. The top was down (he's a convertible kinda dude!) and our family was jamming to my latest iTunes purchases, when a popular pop song came on. Without hesitation, I sang every note, fist bumped and danced without a care in the world while the wind blew through my hair.

About halfway into the second verse, my Dad pulled into a gas station. As he hopped out of the car, he said something that made a lasting mark on my heart: "Emily, I'm surprised you like this... this sounds like it goes against everything you say you stand for."

I stopped dead in my tracks. He was so, so right. I had engaged with something that seemed fun and harmless without even hearing what I was belting at the top of my lungs and consequently, what I was promoting.

The purpose of this chapter isn't to bash a song, artist, or pop culture. It's a reminder to protect my heart and fill my mind with only what my lips preach.

I encourage women to be confident in who they are.

I affirm women in their natural beauty.

I partner with women to become who God made them to be.

I pray for a strong, warrior stance—to be a positive force to be reckoned with.

I fight for healing and grace and combat the lies of shame.

I scream, *You. Are. Enough.*

My car jam session didn't quite line up with what my heart beats for. And that wrecked me. I can't even listen to that particular song in the same light anymore. And it's not even the superficial lyrics that I'm broken over. It's the condition that my heart was in—I had no idea my actions were saying something so divergent from my writing, my passions, my prayers. And that's not a place I want to live.

So, how am I keeping a constant gut check on the connection between my lips and my heart?

I don't see every new movie, jam to every hit song, or read every bestseller. It may seem picky, it may seem silly and it may even seem naive, but when it comes to protecting the deepest chambers of my heart, I'm choosing to not take that lightly. If it's not something I would be comfortable watching with my Dad, singing with my Mom, or talking with my sister about, it probably isn't a healthy decision for me.

Accepting that what may be okay for her may not be okay for me. Each of us struggles with something different. And that's completely okay. But it's not okay to choose to go along with the popular majority on a movie choice you know isn't best for your own heart in an attempt to fit in or be accepted. I'm not arguing with friends and peers about choices I make or decisions they choose. At the end of the day, our connection points between our hearts and actions are between us and God. I'm simply choosing the best yes for me.

I'm staying accountable. I'm on a family Amazon Prime plan, my family has the passwords to my social media accounts, and I share what I'm doing with my time with them on a daily basis. I don't do this because I'm not trustworthy, but because I have nothing to hide—and I want it to stay that way.

I want the words I write, the prayers I pray, and the words of encouragement I offer to align with everything I do—even down to the entertainment choices I choose. Who I am and how I interact with the world is the one variable I have control over. I can't control what happens to me, but I sure can control what happens in me. And this girl? She simply wants to live a life where her words, thoughts, dreams, passions, and calling collide into a beautiful masterpiece.

How are you keeping your media choices aligned with your heart?

dear me: lessons learned.

"You must do the things you think you cannot do."
- Eleanor Roosevelt

Dear me,

In your 29 years, you've learned, traveled, made big moves, and experienced some pretty incredible things; but perhaps the most incredible "things" are the lessons learned along the way.

As you wrap up this 29th chapter of your becoming story and step into a new decade—30!—remember these 29 lessons learned (maybe these notes-to-self can help you out too, warrior friend).

1. You are becoming. God designed you to live in process, not to strive aimlessly for perfection.
2. You know who you want to be… you just have to choose to be her.
3. You are a warrior.
4. Peace is choosing to stand rooted in trusting Jesus regardless of what is happening to you or around you.
5. Being right is highly overrated.
6. Without information, you can't make informed decisions—so ask questions. Always ask questions.

7. Don't date for potential. Be with a man who challenges you in the best way and always encourages you to become who God made you to be.
8. Family is the most important relationship. Value them. Cherish them. Family can be the people you choose to be family, too.
9. There are no regrets, only learnings—moments, relationships, and situations shape, mold, and help you become who God made you to be.
10. That little blog you started as a part of a contest you didn't win? It will change your life and thousands of people you may never even meet face-to-face on this side of eternity. Don't quit.
11. A simple email to a woman you admire will change your life too. Little did you know pushing "send" on that email as a high schooler, that you would begin a lifelong friendship and mentorship with Jenni Catron.
12. Never stop learning. When you do, you're dead.
13. Don't underestimate or undervalue your health. Life is precious... set good habits today that will set you up for success tomorrow and years from now. You'll never look back and wish you'd have slept in; you'll look back with pride at the strength it took to get up.
14. Don't limit yourself... always set yourself up with options. Don't place everything in just one opportunity; be open to many opportunities.
15. Collect many moments, memories, relationships and learnings, not things.
16. Get rid of all the excess. Clean out the clutter, unsubscribe, and unfollow. The things and voices you invite to be an intimate part of your story matter.
17. Don't be afraid to try. You'll always learn something new—and something new about yourself.

18. Steward the resources God gives you and be generous. Save, save, save.
19. Embrace delayed gratification... timing is everything.
20. Being comfortable and confident in your own skin is the best make-up.
21. Before you can really love others, you must first love yourself.
22. Don't be afraid to get messy—dive into the gritty, hard work. It usually always ends up being the most rewarding and satisfying.
23. People pleasing is a lose-lose dead end... and it usually always leaves you disappointed in the long run. Be you for you, not for anyone else.
24. Wherever you are, be all in. Get involved in your community and always choose to be a solution maker, contributing to the place and people you call home.
25. Don't put such high expectations on people. You're just setting them up to fail. Trust God, and from there, love people for who they are. And... don't put unrealistic expectations on yourself either. Walk rooted in and extend grace.
26. Embrace the process; there is protection in the waiting.
27. Do the work of getting to know how you're wired—the Enneagram is an invaluable tool in discovering when and how you're moving in health and when you're moving in stress. Become a student of you and never stop growing.
28. Pause. Take a breath. It's not always as serious as you think it is.
29. In Christ, you fight from victory, not for victory.

And in the midst of all the lessons learned, never forget the most important truth of all: Jesus is first. Don't skip time with Him. He is everything. He is good and He can be trusted.

Time rooted and grounded in Him is the secret sauce to becoming who God made you to be.

Here's to the truths experienced and learned in the first 29 chapters... may the journey continue.

Keep becoming,

when you feel uninvited.

"It's impossible to hold up the banners of victim and victory at the same time."

- Lysa TerKeurst

It was a normal day, until it didn't feel so normal. I was scrolling quickly through Instagram, liking friends' posts, when after double tapping one post in particular, I did a double take. *Wait a minute. Wasn't this the friendship outing I had suggested to my friends not too long ago?* Pause. Take a breath. Double check who posted the picture in the case it wasn't even one of the friends I mentioned this activity to...

My second look confirmed my heart's ache—my friends had gone to the event I suggested and didn't invite me. In that moment, I felt crushed. I felt unseen, unimportant, uninvited.

In the midst of my hurt, I began writing a plot line in my head—*they don't like me; they didn't want me to go; they thought they'd have more fun without me; I'm no fun; I don't have friends.*

And then a second thought crossed my mind—*Emily, they didn't even think about it. It completely escaped their minds. They weren't intentionally not inviting you. And maybe they did. But truly, does it matter? Would you have been able to go on that day* anyway?

It was at this crossroads of attitudes that I knew I had a decision to make. I could either live in the fiction I was creating, or I could embrace the plot line of God's truth. But I couldn't embrace both.

I love this line (and gut wrenching truth!) from Lysa TerKeurst's book, *Uninvited*: "It's impossible to hold up the banners of victim and victory at the same time." I knew in my heart as I sat with my phone in my lap that this was true. I couldn't walk away from the post I saw (or the feelings I felt) in victory if I played the victim card. Did that change the stinging sensation I felt? No. Did it change that I was uninvited? Not at all. But it changed my posture towards it.

I began to ask myself several intentional questions:

Emily, were you available to hang out the day your friends went to this event? No.

Emily, with everything else on your calendar at that time, would you have wanted to go to the event? No.

Emily, did your friends ever tell you, "We don't like you, so you're not invited." No.

With each answer to my questions, I breathed a little deeper, a little more calmly, and allowed the truth to soak my heart with grace. I don't know whether my friends intentionally or unintentionally didn't invite me, and that's okay. I'm choosing to fill in the gap with grace because there have certainly been many moments in my own story when I've forgotten to invite someone, text a friend, send that card, or say "thank you." I've made others feel uninvited and it's never been intentional. In those moments, I would want my friends and those around me to extend grace to me, too.

If you haven't read Lysa TerKeurst's book *Uninvited* yet, run to Amazon to order your copy. It. Is. Gold. I value how Lysa infuses each page with her story and experiences and shares tangible next steps for what to do when you feel uninvited. Chapter 11 is one

I've held onto with both hands and keep close for moments like my Instagram-scrolling-turned-into-feeling-uninvited moments. In this chapter, Lysa shares *10 Things You Must Remember When Rejected*. Have your placed your Amazon order yet? This book will be a help and resource on your becoming journey.

Does feeling uninvited sting? Oh yeah. But what I choose to do with the sting defines what happens next... and ultimately how I choose to live in the feelings of being uninvited, or become the victor over those feelings, determines how I'm becoming who God made me to be.

Warrior friend, we all have moments when we feel uninvited. Don't live there. Look beyond this moment into the truth: you are enough, there's nothing wrong with you, and the best is yet to come. I'm choosing to believe that deep down inside my core. Will you join me?

being authentic in a filter-covered world.

"Sometimes we motivate ourselves by thinking of what we want to become. Sometimes we motivate ourselves by thinking about who we don't ever want to be again."

- Shane Niemeyer

I'll never forget one day in particular as a high school student, walking through the hallway of my church, and my youth pastor saying, "Hey, Emily! How are you?" I wasn't having a stellar day, yet out of habit, I plastered a smile on my face and replied, "Hey! I'm good. How are you?"

Immediately recognizing I was not "good," I was faced with a decision: would I protect my answer with a glossy filter, or would I scrub my filtered answer clean and share the truth?

In that moment, I faced a crossroads I've experienced many different times in my becoming story. It's far too easy to place filters on our lives—from covering up the acne breakouts you're wondering why you still get long past puberty; to consuming obsessive amounts of coffee to hide the fact that you didn't get a full night's sleep; to texting a million happy face emojis to that friend who hurt your feelings to hide the fact that you really do feel hurt; to spraying Febreeze frantically inside your car before carpooling with a friend to hide the lingering smell of spin class; to playing it cool when the guy you've been crushing on asks another girl out on a date. We have multiple moments each day (or, every hour) when our stories, lives, and cars beg for cover-ups. And are all filters bad? No—making your car smell better is definitely a good thing! The danger comes when we cover who we are with a filter of who we think we should be. As a result, when we live a filtered life, we miss out on being who God designed us to be.

That day in high school, faced with answering a simple question, I discovered that #NoFilter living is done best when you throw out your default, safe answer, and share what's really going on in your world. Debating my answer, I stopped in my tracks. I looked my youth pastor in the eyes and said, "Actually... I'm not so good today." I didn't offer an explanation and he didn't ask for one... in fact, I don't even remember what he said after that. But I'll never forget that I peeled back the filter and authentically shared the truth.

Authenticity is recognizing the moments you're not choosing to be who God made you to be and course correcting, making a 180-degree turn and choosing to be her instead of faking it. That, my friend, is choosing to lace up your warrior boots and fight to become who God made you to be.

Life's not perfect. We're not perfect. I'm not perfect... and I never will be. What I'm discovering is that I don't need to compete with that girl on social media or make my life look like a pretty version of what I think success is. I just need to be me. That is success.

So, does living unfiltered mean you literally walk around 100% *unfiltered*, saying anything that pops into your mind and doing whatever you feel like doing, not caring what those around you experience? Not at all. Living authentically is living rooted in wisdom, knowing who you are and Whose you are. There is wisdom in *not* always sharing *everything* with *everyone*. Sometimes the best unfiltered thing you can do is choosing to hold your tongue, not tweeting that opinion, texting that response, posting that photo, going to that event, hanging out with that friend, or saying "yes" to that opportunity. Sometimes the most authentic thing you can do is say "no" because it's the best decision for *you*.

So on the days that aren't so good, I'm choosing to not cover up my bleeding heart. That doesn't mean I shout from the rooftops, "Hello world, my day stinks!" and turn my Instagram feed into a cry for attention; however, it does mean that the people in my inner circle will be invited into what's taking place inside my mind and heart, and in sharing, I'm not only giving the world—but I'm giving myself—the gift of #NoFilter living, choosing to be me.

> Make a careful exploration of who you are and the work you have been given, and then sink yourself into that. Don't be impressed with yourself. Don't compare yourself with others. Each of you must take responsibility for doing the creative best you can with your own life.
> (Galatians 6:4-5, MSG)

throw grace around
like confetti.

friends & frenemies.

"You are the average of the five people you spend the most time with."

- Jim Rohn

For too long, I was on a never-ending quest for that one, perfect best friend. You know what I'm talking about—that girl you're joined at the hip with, who you tell all your secrets to, who finishes your sentences, knows your favorite Starbucks drink without having to ask, and who with a single twitch of her eyebrow can communicate an entire conversation's worth of information. Yes, that girl.

And then on my 24th birthday I decided to put my car in park, ditch society's scavenger hunt to a BFF, and start really looking at the women already around me.

As if I was seeing for the first time, everything around me took on new life, new meaning, new purpose. Up until that point, I had been searching so fervently for one BFF, that I was missing the many incredible people right in front of my eyes.

We are human. We're going to mess up, fail, and let each other down. That's just a part of life. But somewhere along the way, between the kindergarten playground and classic Hollywood college friendship duos, we began hoping for something a little different in our friendships—someone that would make us feel better about ourselves, not alone, and like someone out there really knows us and cares. Not all of the reasons we began the BFF quest are off-base. However, anytime we seek to be filled and made whole by another human, we're going to fall short, be left disappointed, and feel more broken than we felt before.

People don't complete us. Another human does not define me or determine my worth. That's already been established by the One who created me (Romans 9:25, Deuteronomy 7:6, John 1:12, Psalm 139, Isaiah 49:16, Isaiah 43:1). Relationships are meant to complement who we already are and challenge us to become who God made us to be.

Throughout my friendship wins, flops and frustrations, I've come to discover three myths that I've believed along the way and why they're not true:

Myth #1: One person will complete me.

We were made to do life together, not search for one person to complete us. Our friendship "success" rate isn't based on the number of inner circle companions we have, but rather on the depth of those relationships and who we're becoming in light of them. You aren't less of a person if you don't have that "one" best friend. You are a fun, amazing woman who is deeply valued and cherished by God. Your Creator sets your worth, not another member of His creation.

Myth #2: Friends are forever and ever.

Sometimes friendships are for a season and that's okay. Have you ever found yourself looking around your circle of friends and discovering that you were missing a face or two who had been journeying with you? We all experience different chapters in our lives, and with those chapters come both new and old characters—and sometimes, characters make an exit from our story entirely. While some exits are painful and would be best reconciled by laying down differences and offering grace-soaked apologies, other exits can just happen out of the blue. Friends come and go—and that doesn't necessarily mean that something's wrong, broken or out of place. Our chapters and seasons are constantly changing, whether it be through moving to new cities, updated relationship statuses, kiddos entering the picture, family emergencies, or hectic career projects. As the tides shift and friendships change, thank God for the time you did have with that person and pray blessings over them as they continue becoming who God made them to be. Often when we attempt to force friendships to continue moving forward, we end up not only wearing each other out, but also becoming more frustrated in the process. Let it be. Thank God for who they are and for who you are. And then pour all of your love and attention into who God has placed in your chapter right now—we never know how long we'll have the privilege of traveling with them. Cherish today.

Myth #3: I am the perfect friend, if only I could find someone like me.

You're not a perfect friend either. Have you ever thought, "Um, hello! I am a *really* good friend. I mean, why can't everyone else just see that?" Yeah, nope. We all mess up. We *all* need grace. A lot of it. I'm discovering the healthiest way to step into a friendship is by asking, "what can I learn from (insert name)?", rather than, "what can (insert name) give me?". When I show up to the table more interested in who she is, I, in turn, walk away feeling more blessed, more thankful, and more full of life. I'm not perfect, nor will I ever be. It's time to strip others of the expectation of perfection and strip myself of that expectation, too. Life is too short to pretend we have it all together—when mess-ups happen, own them gracefully and just keep taking the next best step in front of you.

I have never been more satisfied relationally than I have been since I threw these three myths out the window. Now, rather than searching for the other half to my best friend bracelet, I'm getting to know *tons* of fabulous women around me! And that's really cool! I'm also thanking God tremendously for the friends He has blessed me with during different chapters of my becoming story—how they challenged and shaped me, how they helped me grow. And I'm jumping in big swimming pools of grace. I'm stepping into each relationship a broken-down, Jesus girl who's simply excited to link arms with another friend on this journey of becoming me.

So, what happens when you run into a mean girl on the friendship journey? We've met them on the playground, been excluded from their lunch tables, written songs about them, been bruised by their words, and tried wearing pink with them on Wednesdays.

I've always been a fan of the concept of cheering on the women around us. Rather than living in a spirit of competition, why not build each other up—we're all on the same team after all, right? But life doesn't always work that way. We find ourselves coming face-to-face with friends-turned-into-what-seems-like-enemies as we tear each other down and end up feeling like we amount to nothing in the process.

Here's what I know to be true: we've all experienced a "mean girl" at some point on our journeys. We've been hurt, believed less of ourselves, and simultaneously wanted what she had—the popularity, the status, the girl squad, the it factor.

But I also know this to be true: *hurting people hurt people.* The mean girls in my story had their own hurts and heartaches and pain. In the midst of their own grief, they threw their hurt onto me, throwing meanness in an attempt to take down the hearts around them too.

> Don't repay evil for evil. Don't retaliate with insults when people insult you. Instead, pay them back with a blessing. That is what God has called you to do, and he will grant you his blessing.
> (1 Peter 3:9, NLT)

How can we navigate the battlefield of frenemies? How can we live out the words of 1 Peter 3:9 and choose to combat meanness with kindness—believing the best in people and remaining confident in who we are and Whose we are in the midst of harsh words, angry glares, gossip, and backstabbing?

Realize mean girls are hurting too. When the insults are flying, it's really hard to pause and ask, "What's happening in her world—what hurt is she experiencing?" But every single time I've made the choice to ask that question and learn more about why the mean girls in my life are acting the way they are, I always end up feeling compassionate towards them rather than bitter. There are always two sides to every story—and in the case of mean girls, there's always something happening in their lives that we may or may not know about that is influencing how they're working through their own hurts.

Recognize that we've all had our own mean girl moments. We're all human. We all mess up. We all make mistakes. And we've all been the mean girl at some point in our stories—whether it wasn't responding kindly to a parent or sibling, not inviting the new girl to sit with us at lunch, or gossiping about a fellow co-worker. We've all been there and all need to choose to respond with kindness when we're frustrated, insecure, and hurting.

Throw grace around like confetti. When the mean girls in our lives throw hurt around, fling back with grace. Remembering that mean girls are hurting too and recognizing that we've all had our own mean girl moments, choose to extend love and grace—you never know what kind of impact you'll make in the process.

Let it go. Be wise in how you navigate the murky waters of frenemies. Don't over-reach or desperately try to befriend the mean girls in your story, but do choose to be the light of Jesus in your encounters with them. Walk forward confidently knowing who you are and Whose you are, and choose wisely in guarding your heart. Words do hurt and cut deeply—while we respond with grace, it's not wise to become a doormat to those around us. Let the hurtful words and actions go, and focus solely on what is true: you are a daughter of the King, you're made with purpose, your story is headed somewhere and you're going to be ok. While mean girls are characters that enter our stories, they don't have to take the leading role in our stories.

Hurting people hurt people. But the cycle can break with us. We don't have to walk through the chapters in our stories filled with frenemies with angry fists and broken hearts. The mean girls in our stories don't define us—God defines us. We can thrive even in the midst of heartache and frustration—but only when we choose to lace up our boots and stand firm, walking confidently in our identity in Christ.

> You're familiar with the old written law, "Love your friend," and its unwritten companion, "Hate your enemy." I'm challenging that. I'm telling you to love your enemies. Let them bring out the best in you, not the worst. When someone gives you a hard time, respond with the energies of prayer, for then you are working out of your true selves, your God-created selves. This is what God does. He gives his best—the sun to warm and the rain to nourish—to everyone, regardless: the good and bad, the nice and nasty. If all you do is love the lovable, do you expect a bonus? Anybody can do that. If you simply say hello to those

who greet you, do you expect a medal? Any run-of-the-mill sinner does that. [48] "In a word, what I'm saying is, Grow up. You're kingdom subjects. Now live like it. Live out your God-created identity. Live generously and graciously toward others, the way God lives toward you."
(Matthew 5:43-48, MSG)

5-4-3-2-1-GO.

"Nothing is impossible; the word itself says, 'I'm possible!'"
- Audrey Hepburn

Have you ever just felt... stuck? Stuck in a habit, thought, pattern, relationship, or attitude?

I'm just a little OCD about double checking the doors and windows are locked. When I was a little girl, I vividly remember beginning this silly routine where each night before I went to bed, I would double check that the doors and windows were locked... and then I'd triple check.

Now, in my thirties, I still find myself double and triple checking. A silly habit begun as a kid after watching a scary movie or news clip has morphed into a habit I can't seem to break.

Is this bad? Not necessarily.

Ensuring you're safe is a good thing. However, when a habit or mental pattern masters you, rather than you mastering it, it's a compulsion.

On my becoming journey, I don't want to relinquish control

to anything or anyone other than what God can do in me. I don't want to be controlled by thoughts, feelings, food, substances, people, or even childhood routines like triple checking the locks. I want to walk in the freedom of being unstuck.

2 Corinthians 10:5 says "...we take captive every thought to make it obedient to Christ." We take every thought. Not just one or two thoughts, but every, single thought. As I read this verse, my mind drifts to every little place not controlled by Jesus—my frustrated response to a friend; my feelings of insecurity when I wasn't invited to that event; my anger at injustice; my temptation to turn to food to make me feel better; and, yes, my compulsion to making sure I've locked the doors even when I know they're secure.

So, how do I combat the junk that seeps into my mind? Both the ugly and the not-so-ugly that compete for first place, above Christ?

5-4-3-2-1.

My Dad first introduced me to Mel Robbins, one of the most sought-after speakers in the world, best-selling author and creator of the 5-Second Rule. Mel coaches, "If you can count 5 – 4 – 3 – 2 – 1, you can change your life."

This story is true of Mel's life. Finding herself at rock bottom, completely stuck, she watched on TV one night as a space shuttle prepared for take off. *5-4-3-2-1, BLAST OFF.* As she watched the shuttle take off for outer space, she resolved, *tomorrow, I'm going to get out of bed and begin taking my best next step by counting backwards, 5-4-3-2-1.* Those five tiny numbers changed Mel's entire life. And they're changing mine too.

Mel shares truth: "Change is simple. The problem is us—we make it complicated." In my door-checking addiction, the change agent is simple: I just need to stop double checking the locks. Embracing 2 Corinthians 10:5, I am taking my habit captive, applying the 5-Second Rule, and 5-4-3-2-1 changing.

The same is true for anything in our lives—whether you feel trapped in an unhealthy relationship; overspend on items you know you don't need; are living with your boyfriend even though you know it's not best; reach for the bag of Oreos when you feel at an emotional low; hitting snooze on your alarm even though you promised your workout partner you'd meet them at the gym... the list goes on. Wherever you find yourself today... 5-4-3-2-1 GO. Grab ahold of 2 Corinthians 10:5 with both hands and stop making change so complicated.

Lace up your warrior boots and take your next step. And then the next and the next.

rooted in Christ
I rise, lionhearted.

lionhearted faith.

"Let us live in such a way that nothing is bigger than our awareness of God's presence in our lives."

- Anonymous

For a tiny five-letter word, faith feels somewhat intricate and knotted to me. There were moments growing up in the church when I heard words like "faith," "believe," and "trust" and began equating them with action steps and calculated outcomes rather than a relationship built on the bedrock of what I believe. And that was one of my biggest misconceptions. What I'm discovering today is that faith was never about following a set of rules or expectations or checklists. Faith boils down to what I actually believe about God.

In the past, when I've read Hebrews 11, I've looked at the stories of the men and women of the Bible and wished I had the guts of their "by faith" moments. I viewed their stories through a lens of fiery action and mighty slingshot slinging—men and women who suited up for battle and charged, bellowing their battle cry. Yes, these individuals did take action, kick butt, and take names; however, they didn't act from a posture of a "let's get this done" mindset. Rather, they acted upon their faith, their deep-rooted confidence in God.

I've had faith all wrong. I thought faith was measured in active points—that if I really believed God is who He says He is, I would invite strangers to church, sell all of my belongings and move to a third world country, or live on Ramen noodles so I could give more than I took. While those aren't bad things—they aren't the litmus test for whether we have faith or not.

So, what really is faith? The dictionary defines it as "*confidence* or *trust* in a person or thing."

The Bible defines faith as:

> The fundamental fact of existence is that this **trust** in God, this faith, is the firm **foundation** under everything that makes life worth living. It's **our handle** on what we can't see.
> (Hebrews 11:1, MSG, emphasis added)

> It was what he **believed**, not what he **brought**, that made all the difference.
> (Hebrews 11:4, MSG, emphasis added)

Faith isn't about doing, it's about being—being so grounded in relationship with Jesus that everything else flows from trusting Him. Faith is the bedrock from which we build everything else. Simply put, faith boils down to our belief system—do we believe God is who He says He is? Do we trust that He has a plan for our lives? Do we trust Him to see us through?

The litmus test to our faith lies within our answers to those questions. Faith is marked by what we believe about God.

Take a few minutes to answer this question: Who do you believe God is?

As I wrestle through this question, here's what I know to be true: when I believe God is who He says He is, everything changes. I'm confident in who I am and who I'm becoming; I have hope for today and a promise for tomorrow; I believe I am created with purpose, on purpose; I can love people no matter what they do or don't do because my trust is in God; I release my worries to Him because God is greater than my fear; rooted in Christ I rise, lionhearted.

What we believe about God is the ultimate game changer. If we don't truly believe He is God and He is good—even when everything around us is in shambles—then we're just going through the motions, putting on a pretty mask, sipping our lattes, checking Sunday church experiences off our weekly to do lists, and wondering why nothing is really transforming in our lives. A lionhearted kind of faith embraces that this world we live in is messy and broken, but God is good and He can be trusted—and He has equipped us for battle and empowered us to become the lionhearted people He made us to be.

So warrior friend, who do you believe God is? Are you ready to lace up your boots and really ask yourself that question? When we do, it unlocks everything.

becoming ana.

This chapter was written by a fellow warrior with you in mind.

Pursuer for the next accolade. Perfectionist. People pleaser. Overachiever. Onlooker of the greener grass. Obsessor of avoiding failure.

As the girl who always got straight A's, always aimed to do the right thing (and probably, too many things), those are just a few descriptions of who I thought I was before I met Jesus—which led to my identity completely shifting and knowing who I truly am in Him.

Now, let me quickly rewind—I discovered at a young age that achievement quickly accumulated praise, and making errors seemed to quickly accrue disappointment. In perfect Enneagram 7 fashion, I thought, *why not soak up as much good as humanly possible?* Starting with good intentions, this mindset led to an unhealthy desire for control, a dream of becoming a lawyer just because everyone else wanted that for me, an eating disorder in my teens, and a non-stop pursuit of fleeting happiness—although I had no actual working definition for what happiness was.

By God's grace, at the age of 13, a friend invited me to a summer camp at UCLA—my dream law school. Boys, beach, and where

I want to get my bachelor's degree? Yes please. Looking back, I think my friend tricked me and didn't give full context as to what the church side of camp entailed, but I'm incredibly grateful because that camp led to the salvation of my soul.

That was almost 14 years ago, but I'm still on the journey of becoming who God made me to be. I've learned that the imperfect parts of my story I so deeply wished I could erase have become the highlight moments for ministering to other people and truly illustrating what Jesus has done for me, can do for them, and who I am becoming in Him.

No longer am I becoming the subpar dreams I had or the 50-year plan I sketched out, but I'm becoming Ana in Jesus. What does becoming Ana mean exactly? It means I'm focusing on what it means to live and lead like Jesus, and not letting any setback hold me back from that intention, but actually propel me into them. It means I'm examining what God is looking to invest into my soul, and how who I'm becoming will help other people know Him and allow the Church to flourish.

For my entire life, the question has been: Despite who I'm becoming, what am I supposed to do? Yet, through His grace, the question constantly on my heart, mind and soul is: Despite what I'm doing, who am I becoming?

I invite you to ask the same question. Despite your failures or setbacks or the parts of your story you wish you could erase (which I'm certain God can and will use someday to help you fly)... in spite of what you're doing, who are you becoming?

warrior steps.

(1) What step(s) are you taking today to trade your Martha mindset for a Mary heart?

(2) How will you keep a constant check on the connection between what you say and what your heart beats for?

(3) What are some of the top lessons you've learned on your becoming journey so far? Write them down!

(4) How will you choose to respond when you feel uninvited? Will you choose to live in the feelings of being uninvited, or will you choose to become the victor over those feelings... choosing to be who God made you to be?

(5) What does it look like to give yourself—and the world around you—the gift of #NoFilter living, authentically being who God made you to be?

(6) Which of the three friendship myths have you believed in the past? How will you step into freedom, embracing the truth of how to be a friend to those around you?

(7) What do you need to 5-4-3-2-1-GO! today, lacing up your warrior boots and taking the next step... and then the next step... and the next?

(8) Who do you believe God is? Are you ready to lace up your warrior boots and really ask yourself that question? When you do, it unlocks everything. When your hope is rooted in Christ, God is WITH you, He is IN you, and He is FOR you. A personal relationship with God changes EVERYTHING. Warrior friend, if you don't have a personal relationship with God, email me at emily@becomingme.tv. I'd be honored to introduce you.

your story matters.

"One day you will look back and you will be able to see: so many little things came together in ways you were not expecting."
- Morgan Harper Nichols

we all have a story.

"'For I know the plans I have for you,' declares the Lord, 'plans to prosper you and not to harm you, plans to give you hope and a future.'"

- Jeremiah 29:11, NIV

For the longest time, I didn't think I had a story—or at least, not an interesting one to share. Growing up as a pastor's daughter, I was introduced to Jesus early on and have always felt a passion for living boldly deep within my heart. As those around me shared their experiences, their moments of experiencing the radical grace of God, I unintentionally compared their life change with mine and concluded that my story just wasn't all that compelling. I began to think that my story wasn't good enough—wasn't good enough to share, and wasn't good enough to help others.

Sometimes I wish I had one defining moment I could pinpoint where everything just clicked, and I realized just how important my story really is. But that's not quite how my paradigm shifted. My thoughts, perspective and attitude towards my own radical grace story changed as BecomingMe.TV shifted into what it is today. This growing resource and community started as a personal blog, documenting my becoming story. Everything both for

BecomingMe.TV and my journey changed when I invited other women to share their voices, too.

Listening to the stories around me taught me the importance of my own story. And this time, rather than place my story side-by-side next to theirs, I simply listened. Don't get me wrong, it wasn't easy at first. I had to consciously tell myself to ask questions and look past the mere words the individual in front of me was sharing, and into their eyes.

That's what made the difference for me.

In their eyes I saw hope. I saw redemption. I saw peace. I saw purpose. I saw becoming. I didn't see a perfect person who had it all figured out. I saw a person embracing who they are and Whose they are, an individual not afraid of yesterday, and someone willing to dive into the depths of their pain. The individual in front of me was a precious daughter of the King of Kings and it didn't even matter what story she was sharing because she was sharing *who she is* with me and that takes courage and bravery and the heart of a warrior.

So I began sharing my story with the eyes looking back at me, too. I shared how Jesus is transforming me, how I'm experiencing radical grace, how I'm becoming the Emily God made me to be. I shared *who I am* and in doing so, realized that I do have a story—I have a story that matters because it shares with those around me the woman I am and the woman I'm becoming.

There is not a cookie cutter for stories. We *all* have a story. We all have something to share because Jesus is working in each and every one of us. He doesn't solely work through those who have experienced the traumatic extremes of life. And He doesn't solely work through those who haven't experienced any of the horrors others have. He is weaving each and every one of our stories into a beautiful tapestry. He uses *all* of our experiences for good, for His glory, to shape us into the people He made us to be.

The tragedy in my original assumption that I didn't have a story to share was that, in doing so, I discounted the pain, joy, shame, and heartache I've journeyed through. God has and *is doing* an incredible transforming work in my life, I just need to look up to see it. When I'm so busy comparing my experiences with others and trying to measure up to an invisible "story standard," I completely miss out on what God is doing right here, right now, and I miss out on the joy of celebrating what He has brought me through. Because we have all looked fear and pain and tragedy in the face in one form or another. We have all had to choose to be a warrior or the victim. We have all walked onto the battlefield of life. We each carry pain and we each carry tremendous joy. And we are all becoming who God made us to be.

This is why I love BecomingMe.TV's Becoming Stories. These stories allow us to look into the eyes of warriors and listen as they share who they are and who they're becoming. These women and men bravely share their hearts, their insecurities, their fears, and their victories. That's what I want to celebrate. Because when I look at these warriors, I can't help but think about how incredible they are simply because they chose to use their voice to share their story and empower the people around them to do the same.

Over the past few years, I've received countless emails, Facebook messages, Twitter and Instagram DMs, emails, and text messages from people sharing their experiences, sharing what they're learning and who they're becoming. And every time I open one of these messages I can't help but smile and then cry just a little because of the beauty pouring forth. There's nothing more beautiful than when we realize we don't have to be ashamed of who God made us to be, but rather that we should share who we are with the world around us.

Warrior friend, you and I have incredible stories to share. We just need to have the courage to raise our voice, stop comparing our stories, lift our eyes, and celebrate who we are with those around us.

I'm going to embrace what happens in the seconds between my fear and my faith taking root.

sharing your story.

"Use me, God. Show me how to take who I am, who I want to be, and what I can do, and use it for a purpose greater than myself."
- Anonymous

Every time someone asked me to share my story, I used to start sweating instantly. My mouth would go dry. Words clattered around boisterously in my brain. And then suddenly, as if someone had just wrapped a warm blanket around my shoulders on an icy day, peace enveloped me.

In the seconds between shaky knees and peace that passes all understanding, something significant happens. God meets me in my mess and reminds me of the truth I so often offer those around me: *Emily, this is your story and your story is what makes you who I created you to be. It's in you. I birthed it in you. You can't mess it up.*

I can't mess it up.

Warrior friend, you can't mess up sharing your story either.

So, now I plunge head-first into the deep end, laying the contents of my heart on the table. I share my pain, my past, my fears. I rejoice in the celebratory chapters and thank God for His radical grace in the tumultuous seasons. I take the next step in front of me, even though I can't see the end of the trail. And therein lies the beauty of becoming—placing one foot in front of the other, trusting God step-by-step on this grand adventure called life.

I'm beginning to get just a little more comfortable with the process of laying the puzzle pieces of my life on the table. It isn't always easy, but sharing who I am never leaves me dissatisfied—in fact, each time I share the contents of who I am with those around me, I always leave feeling thankful, blessed, and whole.

Throughout this nerve-racking process, I've been learning a handful of quick tips and tricks that help me share my journey of becoming who God made me to be:

Write it out. Map out the contents of your story. What are the threads that make you who you are today? Knowing what has happened in each chapter of my journey helps me to visually see my story and provides a fresh perspective for each point and place along the way.

Ask someone to share their story with you. Hearing other people share their becoming stories inspires and challenges me to do the same. As I look into the eyes of the person in front of me, their bravery and transparency beckons me to be courageous too.

Know what you want to share and what you don't want to share. Sharing our stories doesn't mean we automatically resign to living with all of our emotions, decisions, hurts and hang-ups on our sleeves. Decide what components of your story you want to share and which components are just for you, God, and trusted advisors. Sometimes the healthiest thing we can do for both ourselves and those around us is to not extend every little detail of information. Who you share the intimate details of your journey with matters—before sharing, always ask God if you're in the right place, with the right person and in the right heart posture to share.

Share your story with your 6:00 a.m. people. Who are the people you could call at 6:00 a.m. that would actually answer the phone and be there for you in a heartbeat? Those are your people, your tribe. This group of people may already know your story—but regardless of how much your tribe knows, share your story with them anyways. Practicing sharing who you are verbally with the people who know and love you the most will help boost your confidence to share who you're becoming with the people around you.

Walk in grace. We are always becoming who God made us to be and we'll never reach our final destination until we're united with Jesus in Heaven. On this side of eternity, we'll never be perfect, but we'll always be growing, always becoming. Embrace that. Walk in grace. We don't need to have our stories figured out or tied with a pretty bow before we share them. Sharing our stories is simply a decision to invite fellow travelers on the journey with us, sharing who we're becoming.

The next time someone asks me to share my story and my palms start sweating and my mouth goes numb, I'm going to embrace what happens in the seconds between my fear and my faith taking root. And then I'm going to raise my voice and invite that person on my becoming journey. Because as I share who I am with them, I'm also inviting them to be brave with their own story. And that, well, that's worth it all.

Who will you share your story with today?

how to talk about the hard parts of your story.

"Flowers need time to bloom. So do you."

- Anonymous

We all have difficult chapters in our becoming stories—whether we've walked through a difficult breakup, battled addiction, survived abuse, struggled with depression, received the doctor's report we never dreamed we'd ever hear, lost a loved one... the list goes on. We all walk through painful moments in our stories. The question is, can we ever really talk about them? Can we ever share the hard parts of our stories, and if we do, what good would sharing them do?

I remember having a pretty difficult conversation with my family, my tribe, sharing a hard season in my story with them. Was looking into the eyes of those I love and trust the most and sharing something painful with them easy? Not by any means. It was one of the hardest conversations I've ever navigated. But it was also one of the most healing conversations I've experienced.

In sharing the hard parts of my story, I discovered freedom. I experienced healing. I started to fight to choose to be her again.

I found myself. When we carry the heavy, hard stuff alone, we drown in it. God never designed us to travel this journey solo, He designed us to do life together... even in the hardest-moments-of-your-life chapters.

Here's what I also know to be true: who you share the hard parts of your story with matters greatly. When you share your story, you're entrusting the gift of who you are with someone else. Some chapters are meant for only a trusted few; others are meant to scream from the rooftops to the entire world. Armed with wisdom, discernment, and God's direction, you can pinpoint what chapters are best for your own healing and protection to be shared with a trusted few, and which chapters are for all to see, learn from, and celebrate.

So, how did I navigate having a tough yet freeing conversation with my tribe?

First, I allowed myself to feel the toughness of that chapter. I felt the pain, the emotion, the grief. I cried. I prayed. And after I dried my tears, I picked up my pen and journaled. I wrote my thoughts until I couldn't write anymore. In allowing myself to feel the emotions of that chapter and then spill my thoughts on paper, I gave myself an incredible gift—the gift of being. I allowed myself to process, cry, and step back to see what happened in that season.

Then, I picked up the phone and invited my family into my chapter. And you know what? They listened. They prayed with me. They loved me. The hard stuff didn't make them run full speed in the opposite direction. They stayed. And they helped me continue to process and heal. They reminded me of who I am and who I'm becoming and that I have the power to choose to be her.

Talking about the hard parts of your story is... hard. It's not easy. But warrior friend, when you do share the hard parts of your story with those you trust, you'll discover sweet freedom and the beautiful opportunity to take a step forward into the next chapter.

A warrior friend recently shared this: "You're only as sick as your secrets." Holding the hard, secret stuff closely to our chests hinders us from healing, from moving forward.

> He heals the brokenhearted and binds up their wounds. [4] He determines the number of the stars and calls them each by name. [5] Great is our Lord and mighty in power; His understanding has no limit.
> (Psalm 147:3-5, NIV)

> Forget the former things; do not dwell on the past. [19] See, I am doing a new thing! Now it springs up; do you not perceive it? I am making a way in the wilderness and streams in the wasteland.
> (Isaiah 43:18-19, NIV)

Perhaps your best next step today is to make an appointment with a Christian counselor. Or perhaps your best step is hiring a coach to partner with you in identifying and sharing the seasons of your becoming story. Maybe it's time to invite that friend or family member to coffee and share what you have experienced. Whatever your next step is today, identify the best person to share the challenging moments of your story with, and step into freedom, warrior friend. It's so worth it.

hope in the midst of tragedy.

"Sometimes God allows terrible things to happen in your life and you don't know why. But that doesn't mean you should stop trusting Him."

- Christina Grimmie

As I scrolled through my newsfeed one Saturday morning in 2016, reading the heartbreaking news about the artist Christina Grimmie's death the night before, a USA Today article caught my attention—"The one Christina Grimmie Tweet everyone is sharing." I clicked the article link and couldn't help but blink back tears.

That Friday night, Christina had performed a show in Orlando, Florida, and after the event, sat signing autographs for fans. One fan in particular wasn't looking for an autograph; rather, he pointed a gun at Christina, ending her life. As Christina's family, friends, fans, and the world mourned the loss of a 22-year-old woman pursuing her dream, a tweet Christina posted three years prior on February 21, 2013, went viral and hit the top trending articles on USA Today:

hope in the midst of tragedy.

> "Sometimes God allows terrible things to happen in your life and you don't know why. But that doesn't mean you should stop trusting Him."

In the midst of tragedy and confusion, Christina Grimmie's life points people to the incredible hope we have in Jesus Christ. This is the legacy Christina left and shared with the world—just hours before tragedy enveloped people yet again.

Early Sunday morning, not even 48 hours after Christina's death, a gunman wreaked havoc in an Orlando nightclub, launching one of the worst shooting massacres in U.S. history, leaving 50 dead and 53 wounded.

That Sunday, I found myself scratching my head, wondering *what is happening in the world around me?* Discouraged, confused, sad, and at a loss for words, I was reminded of hope, remembering Christina's tweet—"Sometimes God allows terrible things to happen in your life and you don't know why. But that doesn't mean you should stop trusting Him."

I don't have all the answers. I don't know why a gunman shot Christina Grimmie that tragic Friday night. I don't know why gunman walk into unsuspecting places and massacre men and women, boys and girls.

But I do know this: reaching our communities for Christ is our greatest defense against terrorism. When people have discovered hope in Christ, they don't need to take a gun to a public place and murder someone.

And that's what I've staked my life on. That's why BecomingMe.TV exists. Because in the midst of the hurt and confusion and chaos of this thing called life, there is a real God who sent His Son, Jesus Christ, to die for us and rise again, taking away our sin, soaking us in grace and inviting us to have a relationship with Him. It's in our relationship with Christ—it's in discovering hope in Him—that we're free to become who He made us to be, trusting Him first for salvation and in every situation, loving people, and investing our lives for God's glory.

I think Christina Grimmie understood that. As I look at pictures and watch video clips of Christina living out and pursuing her passion, I can't help but smile seeing a woman passionately pursuing becoming who God made her to be and pointing people directly to Him in the process.

I'm committed to remembering Christina's words, because even when I don't know why, I know God is good and He can be trusted. I know God's not done yet. And I'm committed to partnering with people to discover in Christ we have hope.

warrior cheerleader.

"I'm cheering you on big time as you're becoming who God made you to be, warrior friend!"

- Emily B. Cummins

I can't pinpoint the moment I first used the words "warrior friend" to describe another warrior on this becoming journey, but its impact is forever etched in my mind.

Several years ago at the end of a women's leadership coaching session I was attending, a woman approached me and thanked me for calling her a "warrior friend" months earlier. She shared how those two words empowered her in a deep way to become who God made her to be. It was here, staring back at this woman, that I knew I would continue to specifically name the "warrior friends" around me... both those I know personally, and those I interact with on social media. The names we speak over each other have the power to breathe life or death, encouraging one another as we're becoming, or discouraging for years to come.

I thank God daily for the people woven throughout the pages of my becoming story that have been my "warrior cheerleaders"—the men and women who, because of their consistent encouragement and intentionality, have cheered me on through seasons and chapters, shaping who I am and who I'm becoming. My warrior cheerleaders have spoken life over me, taught me practical life skills, and had my back through thick and thin. They've asked the tough questions, pushed back on me, cried with me in the difficult moments, and celebrated with me through the wins.

I'm thankful for my parents, Mark and Linda. Throughout the various seasons of my life from childhood to my teen years, college, adulthood, and all of the major and minor life changes along the way, their consistency has taught me the importance of trusting God with every fiber in your being; asking questions (lots of them!); loving others no matter what; and never, ever giving up on being who God made you to be. My Daddy taught me how to budget, to do my own taxes, preach the Word of God, lead others, change a flat tire, and never settle for less than God's best. My Mom taught me the value of a good, home-cooked meal, that loving your family is the most important work you will ever do, the power and freedom of owning your thoughts, emotions and feelings; and to laugh at yourself (a lot!). My parents model a love story every day that reminds me to wait for God's best. They are true partners, making each other better along the way. And they've certainly made me better along the way too.

My sister, Katie, has always been the "wild" to my "safe." She's the Enneagram 7 that God knew this Enneagram 1 needed to remember to enjoy the becoming journey. Her laughter, love for life, and passion for who God has made her to be, is a constant source of encouragement. Chapters of my becoming story I know I'll treasure forever include Katie—road trips, sister adventures, and watching how Katie is pursuing becoming who God made her to be up close and personal never cease to inspire and encourage me!

During my season in Las Vegas, I had four warrior cheerleaders fondly recognized as my "Vegas Parents." Darryl and Tracy were my go-to counsel when anything with my car went wrong (and a used 2003 candy apple red convertible in the desert had one or two things go wrong a lot!) and they were always there for me... those people who you know are in your corner, who have your back, who've adopted you as their own, even though you're not related by blood. Patrick and Brett kept me grounded, reminding me of the foundation my parents had instilled in me for the first two decades of my life. They lived right down the road from my apartment complex and were a safe haven for questions, prayer, relationship advice, and a whole lot of fun. God knew in the two years I lived thousands of miles away from my Daddy and Mom, I would need sources of wisdom who would look me in the eyes and remind me to be who God made me to be, just as my parents had always done.

As a high school junior, I emailed a woman in ministry I respected, asking questions desiring to learn from her expertise and experience! As one of the few female Executive Pastors at the time, I craved learning anything and everything I could from women leading the way for younger leaders like myself. Jenni Catron graciously emailed me back answering my string of questions, and welcoming any further questions I had. From that first email throughout my college career, I continued to check in with Jenni, emailing her questions, asking for feedback, and gleaning wisdom from her email mentorship. As God would have it, Jenni moved to the West Coast around the same time I lived in Las Vegas. I reached out, asking to treat her to coffee for an in-person connect. Without missing a beat, she responded, "Let's do dinner!" As I met my mentor face-to-face, I don't even remember touching my tacos that evening as I scribbled her answers to my list of questions. What that 11th grade girl didn't know as she naively emailed Jenni was that this woman would not just answer my questions, but she would invite me into a life-long mentorship. Now—years later—I have been privileged to work with Jenni and The 4Sight Group, traveling with Jenni to leadership coaching sessions across the country; and I have the honor of calling Jenni both my mentor and my friend.

I first met Ana Munoz as she expressed interest in being an intern in the communications department where I worked. After walking through the interview process and her officially becoming my first-ever intern, I immediately knew we were going to be life-long friends. Ana is one of those warrior cheerleaders that never lets too much time go by without checking in on me always asking, "how's your heart?"... and without making me laugh! We've journeyed through big moves together, Netflix-binged entire shows together, asked each other the questions that needed to be asked before major decisions, and are forever in each other's corner, cheering each other on throughout this becoming adventure.

Jackie Brewster has opened my eyes to who I am and who I'm becoming in such a fresh, invigorating way. In the weeks leading to my 30th birthday, I had the privilege of journeying through Enneagram Coaching Sessions with Jackie. Throughout the course of our time together (including a session on my 30th birthday itself!), we unpacked how I'm wired and how I can continue to grow into who God designed me to be. This time of Jackie coaching me, asking me challenging questions, and encouraging me to be me are moments I'll treasure forever.

Amanda Wolfe and I connected on Twitter. Yep, Twitter. Since that first Tweet, Amanda has been a warrior cheerleader for me. From brainstorming what this dream called BecomingMe.TV could look like, to sharing her Becoming Story, writing countless blog posts, driving to Florida to attend in-person the very first Becoming Event in 2016, and designing this very book, Amanda has always been a warrior friend who I can laugh with and be reminded to never stop becoming who God made me to be.

As you've met my warrior cheerleaders, I hope your own warrior cheerleaders have come to mind. We all have people throughout our stories who have helped shape and mold us—people who have helped us become who we are. Sometimes warrior cheerleaders are for specific seasons, and others stay with us for life. No matter the length, I'm thankful God knows we need cheerleaders in our corner.

During my second cross-country move, a song kept popping up on the radio that I would end up dancing along to, singing the lyrics about cheering others on to my co-pilot, my Mom, my cheerleader. When I encourage those around me, naming them "warrior friends," this is the image in my mind—watching them driving the car of their own becoming journey, dancing, singing along to the radio, and enjoying the ride. And as they drive, I hope they know they've got a warrior cheerleader in their corner, cheering them on big time through every mile traveled along the way.

As I love to end my social media posts as one final stamp to remind you: I'm cheering you on big time as you're becoming who God made you to be, warrior friend!

i am becoming!

"Every day in every way, I am becoming."

- Rachel Allene

In 2012, I decided to put permanent ink on my body with my first tattoo. What I didn't know then was that those eight little letters inscribed on my wrist would become the anthem of my life and spark something remarkable in those around me as well.

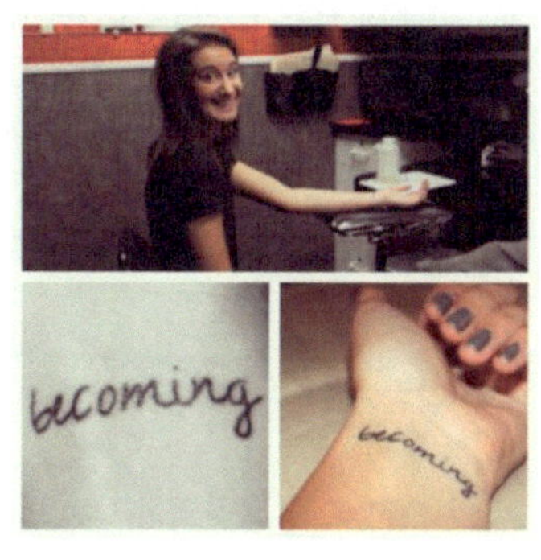

For as long as I can remember, and as I've shared throughout these pages, I've always wanted everything to be perfect. My hair just right. My childhood ballet routines beautifully performed down to the last move. My high school backstroke technique flawless. Perfect A+ grades, never missing an assignment, not even considering doing anything to get a detention. Getting into the right colleges. Choosing the right career. Finding the perfect guy. Making the best of friends. Showing the world I've got it. You know, that *it factor* that everyone seems to want. But, in tear-filled frustration, I always seemed to come up short in comparison to the world's standards. Not pretty enough. Not the star swimmer on the high school swim team. Not the valedictorian of my class. No handsome stud on my side. No group of BFFs I share all of my deepest, darkest secrets with. It's like perfection just wouldn't come—no matter how hard I tried.

And that's when it hit me. *I will never be perfect.* I wasn't created to reach perfection. God created me exactly as He wants me to be—and in His eyes, I am perfectly made. Psalm 139 confirms that. He created me to love and embrace this grand adventure called life; the problem was—and is—that when I was striving so hard to reach what I deemed as "perfection," I couldn't truly live.

The words of Deuteronomy 30:11-14 are empowering me with the truth that I can do what God commands me to do. I don't need to have anyone else explain it to me, teach it to me, or tell me to do it. Obeying God is up to me. I just have to do it. Following verse 14, God lays out some life-altering, eye-opening words that grip me:

> Look at what I've done for you today: I've placed in front of you Life and Good, Death and Evil. [16] And I command you today: Love God, your God. Walk in his ways. Keep his commandments, regulations, and rules so that you will live, really live, live exuberantly, blessed by God, your God, in the land you are about to enter and possess.
>
> (Deuteronomy 30:15-16, MSG)

Live exuberantly. Really live.

I want that. I want to live free of the distractions of wanting to win popularity contests. Free from fighting so hard to be perfect. Free from avoiding messy, real, authentic relationships. Free from being so afraid of getting hurt. Free from trying to avoid failure so intensely. Free from striving to win the approval of others. Free from the icy grip of shame. Free. Free to LIVE.

Each of us are on a journey. Our stories are being written day-by-day, inviting us to become who God made us to be, and

I believe our stories have the potential to really do something, to change the world. But only if we let them.

It really boils down to one thing: who will I trust to write my story? Me or God? Perfection screams, "Choose me! Choose me! Only I can control how everything turns out." But the kind of living Deuteronomy 30 shares whispers the truth, "Choose God. He IS life. If you choose Him, you choose life." When I choose to open my hands and release my grip on false control, I'm no longer striving to "do" anything; I'm simply "being" in His presence, trusting Him to "do" for me that which only He can do.

I am becoming, becoming who God made me to be. Each day a page of my story is being written into the threads of time and being woven into the very fabric of who I am. As I stand looking at the pages before me, I'm making a daily decision to choose to embrace this grand adventure called life, and to trust the God who created me in the first place to continue writing the story of Emily.

I shared as we began this journey together, and I will share this invitation from Shauna Niequist once more to become who God made us to be:

> This season is about becoming [...] walk closely with people you love, and with people who believe God is good and life is a grand adventure. Don't get stuck in the past, and don't try to fast-forward yourself into a future you haven't yet earned. Give today all the love and intensity and courage you can, and keep traveling honestly along life's path.
>
> (Shauna Niequest, *Bittersweet*)

This is why I chose to have "becoming" tattooed to my wrist. Every, single time I look at my left hand, I'm reminded that life is a grand adventure. I'm reminded that the pursuit of perfection isn't what God created me for. I'm reminded that I am made perfectly in Christ. I'm reminded to trust Him to write my story. I'm reminded to live exuberantly. But, most importantly, I'm reminded to embrace becoming me.

And from where I stand today, this idea of "becoming" is permeating everything I do. It's embedded in my writing, engrained in my thoughts, and interwoven in my conversations with those around me. It's taken root as the reason why I get out of bed every morning and the hope I hang on to when the rain clouds come. It's my passion, my heart's cry, my word.

I see people around me becoming who God made them to be, too. I see them courageously battling life's struggles and risking loving people who just might not love them back. I see them trying, setting aside the fear of failure and running towards incredible victory. I see life change. I see redemption. I see courage. I see becoming.

In the Fall of 2014, I attended a Writer's Bootcamp with Margaret Feinberg and Jonathan Merritt. One of the first challenges they posed to their trainees was simply this: what's your mission statement? It was a question I had asked before and tried countless times to define; however, that October, the words came together like magic in a way only God could orchestrate. You see, that eight-letter word I tattooed on my wrist all those years ago has become my mission and I believe the reason God puts air in my lungs.

My battle cry is to invite people on the personal and courageous journey of becoming who God made them to be. That's why I wrote this book. That's why I dream. In becoming me, I see those around me becoming too—I see you becoming, warrior friend—and can't help but be inspired and encouraged on the journey.

This journey isn't just mine. As we've traveled these pages together, my prayer is that you're ready to lace up your warrior boots, choose to be you, and pursue becoming who God made you to be with all you've got. We only have this one, precious, wild, incredible life... let's not miss it, let's not miss out on becoming who we were made to be.

Let's be who God made us to be. Together, let's become.

becoming allison.

This chapter was written by a fellow warrior with you in mind.

To know me is to know I LOVE words—even in their limited capabilities, they allow us to communicate to each other and express ourselves and our stories. Even more, I love double entendres! When I thought of the word 'Becoming'–it made me think of both definitions: 1) (n.) a process to form, to be made into, and 2) (adj.) to compliment, to praise. In my life, I have gained an awareness for how both meanings are resources in my faith journey.

As I've developed more and more in my faith walk, I've learned that the difficult seasons in life are just as vital in working that faith muscle as are the flourishing ones. The hard moments are sometimes where I have experienced the love of God is such a tangible way.

I had the epitome of child-like faith growing up. I believed with all my five-year-old heart that whatever I asked God for, it would happen. Just as certain as I believed my parents would love, care for, feed and clothe me—I knew God would answer just as surely. This mindset stayed with me throughout my life with minimal confusion or questioning. It wasn't until life came as a shattering hurricane that I had to become more aware of how faith worked.

At the end of 2012, my father passed, followed by the loss of my sister a few months later. BAM!! Talk about a gut punch! The world as I knew it, childhood memories as I once told it, family as I once felt it, had disappeared. No one asked my opinion about it; it seemed the world didn't care how this impacted me—what was familiar, had just vanished. Though I was surrounded by people in the height of my shock and grief, I felt alone and abandoned by people I loved so dearly. How could they just be... gone?

The sad part was, it wasn't just loved ones that I had to process the loss of, without realizing it, that full-bodied faith I had was close to depletion. You see, up to that point in my life, my faith was built on the outcome of my prayers going my way. Never in my life had I prayed as hard as I had for my dad and sister—but the story I wrote in my prayers didn't have the outcome I asked for, BUT GOD...

I clung to the verse Psalms 34:18—that God is with the broken hearted. As people loved me, I felt God through them and allowed myself to find peace in that care. I stayed consistent in talking to God. I brought Him my questions, concerns and frustrations and He met me with revelations, peace and understanding. I learned that faith isn't based on the answers to my prayers going my way, it's trusting my Heavenly Father completely. He has ALL THE DETAILS—past, present, and future—and is incapable of withholding good from me. As I grew in these truths, I began to look more BECOMING in Him! I carried trust, faith, and confidence within me and wasn't the same Allison I was before. God is writing each page of my book in His timing. I don't have to hold God to my 'watch' or my timing, I just know that He is watching over me. I find joy in *becoming* the Allison God's designed me to be as He makes me more *becoming*!

warrior steps.

(1) What's your story? Grab a notebook or your laptop and write out what has made you who you are today.

(2) Who will you share your story with today?

(3) What step(s) do you need to take to talk about the hard parts of your story?

(4) Will you commit to choosing to believe that even when you don't know why or understand the circumstances around you, that God is good and He can be trusted? Will you believe the truth that He's not done yet? Talk with God today, asking Him to fill you with courage and commitment to partner with people to discover hope in Him... no matter what we face!

(5) Who are your warrior cheerleaders? Let them know this week by sending a text, card, flowers, surprising them with coffee... say thank you!

(6) YOU ARE BECOMING! What is one takeaway from this book you will apply to your becoming journey?

acknowledgements.

These pages have been eight years in the making and include thousands of miles traveled in the first three decades of my becoming story—big moves, heartbreak, joy, and so many big-little learnings about myself, God, and who He designed me to be along the way. Beginning this journey at 23-years-old, and now publishing *Becoming Me: Choosing To Be You* at 31, my heart is bursting with thankfulness and humility at the privilege of sharing my becoming story.

I am so thankful for the many warriors who have and continue to impact, influence, and invest in me on my becoming journey. I couldn't have pushed publish on these pages without the following warriors... I thank each of them from the bottom of my heart.

First and foremost, God, thank You for creating and designing me uniquely as *Emily Beth Cummins*. I am forever grateful for Jesus' sacrifice for me, Your grace, forgiveness, and inviting me on this grand becoming journey. Thank you for loving & guiding this warrior heart of mine. You are the Author of my Becoming Story.

#TeamCummins, wow. You have journeyed through the ups and downs and every, little moment in-between. Daddy and Mom, thank you for always pointing me to Jesus and challenging me to become who God made me to be with every fiber in my being. I am so thankful God chose me and Katie to be your daughters! Katie, you're the sparkle and joy to my journey and I am thankful God not only gifted me with you as a sister, but also as my best friend. Can't wait to continue adventuring together!

Jenni Catron, thank you for reading and responding to that junior in high school's email and for mentoring me ever since! Your investment in me has been and continues to be integral to who I am and who I'm becoming. Forever thankful for you!

Stephen and Jackie Brewster, thank you for your leadership, influence and friendship on my becoming journey—and thank you for always cheering me on to be who God made me to be! Jackie, thank you for partnering with me to discover how God wired me, find freedom from patterns and mindsets I've held onto for years, and rediscover my purpose with fresh eyes and vision for who I'm becoming. Sure do love Team Brewster! Thank you!

To the OG Becoming Team and the BecomingMe.TV Community, can you believe it?! You've journeyed with me and shared your Becoming Stories since we pushed publish on the very first Becoming Story in 2014… thank you for trusting me and this resource with your stories and cheering me on too!

To my Vegas Parents—Patrick and Brett Detken, and Darryl and Tracy Speers—thank you for adopting me as family during my Vegas season. Your investment in me means more than you'll ever know! I love y'all!

Jud and Lori Wilhite, thank you for investing in me during my time in Vegas. It was an honor serving and learning under your leadership. Your time, care, and love for me is forever cherished. Thank you!

Emily Sison, Allie Reefer, Ana Munoz and my Warrior Momma: your editing on this book was a game changer. Thank you for reading with me, laughing with me, encouraging me, and not letting me give up or quit on this dream to publish a book!

Amanda Wolfe, you brought this book, these chapters, pages and stories to life! Thank you for designing *Becoming Me: Choosing*

To Be You and journeying with me... I treasure your friendship! Thank you! And to Marisa Angelino, Michael Allen, and Caitlyn Pace from the Growco Lab team: thank you, thank you! You are dynamic team of warriors I'm so very thankful for!

Katie Cummins, Amanda Wolfe, Allie Reefer, Ana Munoz and Allison Paige: thank you for sharing your Becoming Stories throughout these pages... you inspire me, warrior friends! Thankful for this becoming journey together!

To my Church of Hope Family: I love you! I've grown up with you over the last 13 years—thank you for both welcoming me to BE who God made me to be and cheering me on in this journey!

Sanibel Island, Idaho, airplanes across the country, the #babecave, and Ocala, thank you for providing inspiration, space to write, edit and write again... writing my Becoming Story in each environment holds special memories in my heart.

Warrior friend, thank you for reading and journeying with me... let the becoming journey continue!

hey warrior friend,

Wow... what a journey we have been on throughout this book! Thank you for reading—my prayer for you is that the pages of this book become a warrior battle cry on your own becoming journey, challenging, equipping and encouraging you to choose to be who God made you to be.

In 2012, I tattooed a little eight-letter word on my wrist that has changed the entire trajectory of my life: *becoming*. More than just a phrase or pretty idea or token of inspiration, becoming is a way of life; a journey we're all traveling on. Embracing my becoming journey has not only empowered others to embrace their's as well, but it has stirred up inside me my heart's cry and life's passion: to partner with people, to cheer them on, to equip them on the journey of becoming who God made them to be.

So this is me. I'm passionate about storytelling, good cups of coffee, and jamming to country music. I'm a University of Florida and College of Central Florida grad. I'm a PK who stayed in ministry. And I love it. I'm honored to serve as the Communications Pastor of a dynamic church in Ocala, Florida, Church of Hope. Watching people find their voice and share their story is why I get out of bed every day. And most importantly, I'm passionately pursuing becoming the woman God made me to be.

I'd love to hear your becoming story and cheer you on too, warrior friend! Let's connect!

I'm cheering you on big time as you're becoming you!
The best is yet to come!

Emily

www.becomingme.tv
@emilybcummins
/emilybcummins
@emilybcummins
emily@becomingme.tv

Made in the USA
Columbia, SC
27 December 2023

29519635R00130

We all fight for something—whether it be fighting for education, health, relationships, career goals, or financial success. Culture preaches we must fight to prove validation, arguing when we reach certain milestones & followers on social media, then we will be deemed successful, we will have arrived. But what if we have it all wrong? What if in fighting for something, we're losing our identity, rather than finding it? What if victory was actually fighting from something else entirely?

In Becoming Me: Choosing To Be You, discover through one woman's journey, the power of self-love, choosing to be who you were created to be, what it means to adopt a warrior mindset, the power in sharing your story, & the reality that this grand adventure of becoming is for all of us.

Warrior friend, you ARE becoming.

Emily B. Cummins is the Founder of BecomingMe.TV a global resource equipping people to become who they were made to be through a growing online community sharing people's Becoming Stories conferences, courses, and resources.

Emily also serves as the Communications Pastor at Church of Hope in Ocala, Florida. When she's not writing or speaking, you can find her soaking up the sun at the beach, running, and savoring a cup of coffee while listening to country music.

becoming
BECOMINGME.TV

Book Design: Amanda Wolfe, Growco Lab
Cover Artwork: BecomingMe.TV
Photography: Katie Cummins

ISBN 979898527420
9 798985 274202